No Quarter

Dale Blair

No Quarter
Unlawful Killing and Surrender
in the Australian War Experience 1915–18

Acknowledgements

This research was made possible through the provision of a grant supplied by the Australian Army in 2001 for which I am grateful. My interest in this subject was, however, sparked by a curiosity that had grown well before that time. I am indebted to Mrs Ollie Taylor who, many years ago, allowed me to read a transcript of her father's radio broadcasts about his experience of capture at First Bullecourt and his subsequent internment as a prisoner of war. His name was Reg Sanders and he was in charge of the 4th Light Trench Mortar Battery during that ill-fated battle. It was that reading which planted the seed for investigating his experience in the broader experience of the AIF. Above all, I am indebted to the patience of my wife, Non, and children, Jane and Joe, who have suffered through (though not without complaint, I might add) my occasional hogging of the computer to type up my research. Thanks also to Sean Young for the assistance he provided during my research at the Australian War Memorial.

No Quarter: Unlawful Killing and Surrender in the Australian War Experience 1915–18
ISBN 978 1 74027 291 9
Copyright © text Dale Blair 2005
Cover © Ginninderra Press & its licensors. All rights reserved

First published 2005
Reprinted 2015

GINNINDERRA PRESS
PO Box 3461 Port Adelaide 5015
www.ginninderrapress.com.au

Contents

Introduction		7
One	The Rules of War	15
Two	Gallipoli – 'the Australian when he fights, fights all in'	23
Three	'Kill every bloody German you see…'	29
Four	'Go on, you haven't killed one yet…'	44
Five	'It's no good, sonny, there are too many of them…'	53
Six	Gerfangener	71
Conclusion		76
Notes		86
Bibliography		93
Index		96

Introduction

In the northern summer of 1916, the term 'ratting' entered the lexicon of Australian soldiers and military writers. It referred to the process of clearing German soldiers from the cellars, dugouts and rubble of the French village of Pozières. It was, according to the official historian, C.E.W. Bean, 'grim sport'.[1] Throw in a phosphorus bomb to flush out the occupants and shoot them down or bayonet them as they emerged. It was a simple and effective method of dispatching the enemy.

Yet consider Bean's description a moment and ask what it revealed of the Australian character:

> Throughout the village could be seen isolated Australians 'ratting' occasional fugitives from the rubble heaps, chasing terrified and shrieking Germans and killing them with the bayonet, or shooting from the shoulder at those who got away, and then sitting on the door-steps to smoke and wait for others to bolt from the cellars.[2]

Are we being invited to share a pride in the nonchalant ruthlessness of the Australian soldier? Are we being asked to accept that such sport, of killing men who are clearly no longer a danger, was acceptable in the 'fury of war'?[3] Prisoners were taken, so we know 'ratting' was not an extreme practised by all Australians at Pozières. In fact, large bodies of prisoners were captured. Bean himself recorded parties of up to twenty or more being brought in by the men.[4]

In his account of 'ratting', Bean provided a context of extenuating circumstances. Having taken the village and begun digging in, the Australians had become targets of some enemy snipers who had taken refuge in or survived in the rubble and cellars of the village during the bombardment and the initial Australian attack. It was this, Bean insinuated, that justified the merciless efficacy of some of the Australians on that occasion, the fact that they had been 'stung by the killing of mates beside them'.[5]

One can certainly understand soldiers being inspired by a thirst for revenge. That in itself does not provide justification for killing men who are clearly placed in a situation where they are incapable of resistance or no longer have a desire to resist. Soldiers knew at the time the demoralising effects of artillery bombardment upon men's nerves and resolve. Most of the Germans with whom the sport of 'ratting' was played had been subjected to days of continuous bombardment in addition to the whirlwind barrage that fell upon them in the two minutes prior to the Australian infantry assault at Pozières. Given the alleged activity of snipers in the ruined village, clearly not all had been reduced to ineffectiveness. The question facing Australian soldiers was how to discern which Germans were the snipers.

Throughout his volumes of the official histories, Bean refrained from seriously judging or questioning Australian attitudes to killing in this manner. His uncritical approach has not always been accepted. The British historian John Keegan considered Bean's treatment of Australians involved in killing prisoners at Passchendaele in 1917 as platitudinous.[6]

The incident Keegan referred to was that involving the death of Captain F.L. Moore, 5th Battalion. When a German pillbox garrison signalled their intent to surrender, Moore moved forward to accept the surrender but was shot down. Moore's men immediately killed the perpetrator and others. The garrison's total extermination was only prevented by the interposition of other officers.[7]

In a footnote about this action, Bean recounted what he considered a 'terrible' incident recorded by Captain W.D. Joynt, 8th Battalion, that took place about the same time in his brigade. Joynt admitted to seeing a group of Australians accepting the surrender of the defenders of the lower level of a double-storey pillbox. As the Germans emerged, a shot was fired from the upper level, where the defenders were unaware of the surrender below, and an Australian was killed. Considering this the 'vilest treachery', the Australians commenced to bayonet all the surrendering Germans. Although Bean described the men as being 'too heated' to realise the facts, it was obvious that, for some, the action was cold and calculated and far from frenzied. Bean included a description of how one Australian who, on preparing to bayonet a German, found his bayonet unattached and proceeded to attach it while his stricken victim implored for his life. With his bayonet fixed, the Australian then killed the defenceless soldier.[8] The calm detachment displayed here was hardly indicative of one 'too heated' to act otherwise. It was a cruel, cynical and deliberate act of vengeance.

In that instance, Bean's argument does not sit comfortably with the facts. Joynt, too, even though he knew the truth of the situation, was far from sympathetic in his postwar account. He reflected a widely held and subsequently entrenched view that Germans defending blockhouses and displaying the 'bad sporting spirit of shooting as long as they were safe and then rushing out expecting mercy' were entitled to none.[9] For Keegan, the Australian behaviour here was an example of unqualifiable 'improper violence'.[10]

How should we interpret the behaviour of that Australian soldier and his comrades? Their actions suggest a group mindset that legitimised their behaviour even though in doing so they were contravening the rules of warfare. That the unfortunate Germans were 'entirely innocent' was patently obvious, yet Bean was still unable to condemn the actions of the Australians. Instead, he adopted a general and passive view that accepted the inevitability of such incidents for which the blame lay with 'those who make wars, not those who fight them'.[11]

In the broadest sense, one can hardly argue with Bean. Simply put, if there was no war, there would be no killing of men either legitimately or illegitimately. Yet by applying such a viewpoint to his discussion of the incident, Bean was avoiding the immorality of it and acting as an apologist for the Australian soldiers involved in the episode.

Keegan's chagrin is easily shared, as such actions raise fundamental questions about the morality underpinning the Australian conduct of war. One must ask whether there exist any circumstances at all that justify the practice of 'no quarter' either through the killing of surrendered soldiers or through the refusal to take prisoners.

Peter Charlton, in his account of the fighting at Pozières and the killing of prisoners there, considered the capability of the Germans to resist or not in such circumstances to be 'a moot point'.[12] He followed by quoting Iven Mackay, the 4th Battalion commander at the time, who stated that some prisoners had taken fright to such an extent at the prospect of crossing no-man's land that '[t]hey had to be killed'.[13] This, in essence, represents the defence of military necessity. It was one favoured in many of the postwar accounts that recorded such incidents. If it was true that some were so terrified as to be immovable, one must ask whether killing them was the only alternative? The rules of war extant at the time clearly demanded that they should have been afforded protection. Yet, how did one move and reason with terrified prisoners?

The humanitarian and idealistic answer to such questions would be that enemy soldiers, so compromised, should always be captured not killed. The more hard-nosed and hawkish view would be that soldiers could not take risks in interpreting the state of the enemy in such situations. Killing them was reasonable and the expectation of rational discernment among soldiers, flushed with the excitement of battle, unreasonable – it was war, after all. This was a standard defence for those involved in illegitimate killing.

While questions of ethics and morality are undoubtedly undermined in war, and particularly in the heat of battle, men did not have to surrender reason or their understandings of right and wrong to it – and, indeed, most did not. Nor did citizens supporting the war have to mutely acquiesce when confronted by knowledge of some of war's brutality.

An unsigned and undated letter held by the Australian War Memorial reveals the abhorrence of one person over alleged atrocities committed by Australian soldiers.[14] The letter was sent to Australian Administrative HQ in London and is worth quoting in full not only because of the extraordinary claims it makes but also because of the principled position the writer adopts.

> Dear Sirs
> I have been told by wounded soldiers in hospitals and walking cases storeys [sic] [of] cruelty [sic] and murder of German wounded and prisoners committed by Australian soldiers. From the evidence I have, there can be no doubt.
> I asked a soldier in Kings College Hospital if [he] had seen any German prisoners he said Yes – he saw some been [sic] brought

in by English Tommies and when they got near the Australians the Australians told the English Tommies to clear or they would kill both of them. The Australians killed the whole of the German prisoners – now this was simply cold blooded murder. [A]nother Australian told me he and another was coming back after a trench raid the other fellow had two German prisoners and they could not get along as fast as they would like so he killed the two German prisoners. Brave men these where [sic] they not – A Canadian told me he (an officer) had seen the Australians jump on the wounded Germans as they lay on the field of battle and told German prisoners to go back [as] they did not want them and when they turned to go back they turned the machine-gun s on them and mowed them down – A A.M.C.A. told me one of his stretcher-bearers carried a razor in his pocket and when he came to a wounded German he would finish him off by cutting his throat and he is still doing it – all these and other men have signed their statements. Disc nos given and names of places where these events took place – I am engaged in collecting evidence from all classes of soldiers both sides not from Govt. statements I have seen some of these and even these prove that the British Army and the Allies are from been [sic] saints or even civilized.

Facts are stubborn things and this book will not be plesent [sic] reading for young Australians or cover those [who] fought in this war with glorey [sic] – I thought if your attention [is drawn] to this matter you might be able to do something to stop the crulity [sic] and murder. For two wrongs don't make a right. We ought to show the Germans we are far above this kind of work. If the men saw the officers were determined to put a stop to it, they would [not] do that wich [sic] spoils the fine work they have done during the war. [A]t present the officers only wink at it the men say and take no steps to stop it.

Yours trully [sic]
A record of Daily Events of the war
May 13th

It would be easy to dismiss the claims as outrageous. The thought that a stretcher-bearer was engaged in slashing the throats of German prisoners seems highly unlikely, given the compassion generally understood to have been extended by men collecting the wounded of friend and foe alike. The possibility exists that the writer was seen as a gullible type and that he was fed fanciful stories that played upon his astonishment. The anonymity of the author also reduces the letter's credibility. Furthermore, the statements being collected, if they were provided, have either been lost in transit, destroyed or are still to be discovered. Nonetheless, the commandant of the Australian Administrative HQ kept the letter for posterity's sake and forwarded it to the Australian War Museum section for preservation, an indication, perhaps, that he did not reject the claims out of hand. One is certainly less sanguine about dismissing the possibility that Australian soldiers could act in such a manner given the incidents Bean portrayed in regard to 'ratting' at Pozières and Captain Moore's death at Passchendaele. The claims, even though ultimately unsubstantiated, are enticing and invite research by modern historians to discover the extent to which they or similar incidents occurred.

It is clear, too, despite Bean's willingness (albeit somewhat guarded) to address the issue officially, that some senior officers of the AIF wished to avoid any controversy that might besmirch the name of Australian soldiers. General Sir John Monash claimed that 'Australian soldiers are nothing if not sportsmen, and no case ever came under my notice of brutality or inhumanity to prisoners'.[15] Brigadier General 'Pompey' Elliot was another keen to distance his soldiers from allegations of unseemly behaviour and penned a rebuttal, in the New South Wales RSL journal *Reveille*, of a claim by Robert Graves that Australian troops had murdered German prisoners at Mourlancourt.[16]

Of particular interest is the correspondence generated between Brigadier General John Gellibrand and C.E.W. Bean in response to an article published in the *Sydney Sun* by the recently repatriated commander of the 9th Brigade, Brigadier General Alexander Jobson (who was elected as president of the New South Wales Returned Sailors' and Soldiers' Imperial League of Australia soon after). Jobson claimed that troops under his command had openly and deliberately ignored the rules of war and practised 'no quarter'. An outraged Gellibrand wrote to Bean doubting the veracity of such claims, stating he had only heard of two cases in the war and both were hearsay. He suggested Jobson had been 'gulled' or was suffering battle strain. 'If it is true,' he wrote, 'it is not typical of our men or officers and it is an abortion of spirit if it is false.' Gellibrand urged Bean to publish a letter celebrating 'the Australian as a fighter, with clean hands and a clean record'.¹⁷ Bean did not provide the unequivocal response that Gellibrand was looking for. He replied, in part,

> Candidly I don't know what to do in that case. I am up against this, that one has so constantly heard our men and officers talk as if these things did happen, and laugh about them, that I am half inclined to think they must have happened more often than we would like to believe. I have never had any first hand evidence of this on either side except in one or two cases; but if the rumour does get round that it happened, at least our men and officers have done nothing to stop the rumour being spread... Whether these things are done or not, one hates the attitude which approves of them, and the publication of them could only excuse the German for refusing to take prisoners from amongst our own men... You see I cannot well come out and say I don't believe that this is done, because I have heard so many wild stories which I don't know the truth of.¹⁸

The rights of the individual soldier who surrenders or has been rendered hors de combat due to wounding or insensibility provide the guiding consideration of this book. An underlying fear of all soldiers, beyond the prospect of death in battle, was to be captured by the enemy. That fate placed them at the mercy of a foe for whom they had little real understanding, an enemy who, in all likelihood, had been previously defined by the loathsome propaganda to which soldiers had been subjected. Capture represented a great unknown. It meant a role transformation from the combative to the passive. It meant removal from a familiar environment to an unfamiliar one. It invoked feelings of humiliation and inadequacy that could erode a soldier's sense of self-worth. While all this was true, it was only so if a soldier survived the first critical meeting with his victorious counterpart. As the vanquished foe, a surrendering or badly wounded soldier was at the complete mercy of his enemy. How that enemy chose to react could mean the difference between life and death. It is that reaction, both by Australian and German soldiers (as recorded by Australians), which is central to this work.

Discussion about Australian soldiers involved in the treacherous act of killing prisoners is usually limited to the story of 'Breaker' Morant during the Boer War. Lieutenants 'Harry' Morant and Peter Handcock were members of the Bush Veldt Carbineers operating in the Spelonken district of the Transvaal during August and October 1901. They were arrested and court-martialled for killing twelve Boer prisoners, and executed on 27 February 1902. They argued that the difficulties of guerilla warfare legitimised the killing of the prisoners and that they were acting in response to verbal orders communicated down the chain of command.[19]

More often than not, the central focus of such discussion within the broader Australian narrative concentrates upon the alleged betrayal of the Australians by the British High Command rather than the immorality of the act itself. In regard to Australia's First World War experience, it is a subject that has not been critically engaged and, as the previously quoted Australian officers suggest, it is a subject that has generally invoked a sense of denial. The purpose of this book is to explore the degree to which Australian soldiers were victims, and/or perpetrators, of acts that extended beyond the rules of civilised warfare as they were understood during the First World War. In doing so, it will investigate men's reactions to capture and behaviour at the moment of surrender. It will explore the degree to which unlawful acts were embedded within the culture of the Australian Imperial Force as well as examining the manner in which such killing has been accommodated or ignored in Australia's First World War story.

One

The Rules of War

Australian soldiers of the First World War did not enter the conflict in a moral vacuum. As a dominion of the British Empire, Australian morality was – as was that of the European states – grounded in basic Christian tenets. 'Thou shalt not kill', a fundamental Christian value acknowledging the sanctity of human life, was codified in most Western societies' criminal statutes. Ironically, it was also this basic expectation of civilian behaviour that soldiers were asked to jettison in time of war.

The generation of Australian males that enlisted in the First World War was also the first to have received the benefits of a broad and compulsory state education. A staple part of the diet in the history of young Australians was the military achievements of the British Empire of which they were a part. The archetypal hero of the time, that permeated not only the history texts but also the literary works directed at young readers, was the muscular Christian version of the British officer. The British officer represented the quintessential gentleman and ideal specimen of British manhood. Underpinning his whole demeanour and conduct was a principle of 'fair play'. This notion of 'fair play' intimated decency, courteousness and compassion that was necessarily extended to one's enemy in the expectation that it would be reciprocated. If war was to be waged, then it ought to be conducted in a manner befitting civilised states – despite the obvious paradox that so-called civilised warfare invites.

'Fair play' was also a quality that underpinned the playing of sport in pre-war Australia and Britain. Sport was deemed a proving ground of men's character. Its use as a metaphor for war was well known and understood at the time. Soldiers recruited from a 'sports mad' and relatively educated society were not unaware of its importance to military conduct on entry into the army. If it was lost on some of those who made up the lower ranks in the Australian army, it was most certainly understood by those who ultimately comprised the officer corps. These men had, in the main, been the beneficiaries of higher education, participated in the pre-war militia and volunteer regiments, and occupied many of the higher public offices in civilian life.

On the battlefield, 'fair play', at least theoretically, was to be extended to the beaten foe. One did not mistreat prisoners.

Historically, consideration for the treatment of prisoners can be traced to ancient times. Prisoners have, over the ages, represented a form of military currency. In ancient Greece and Rome, a prisoner's welfare was sometimes ensured by their value as slaves or labourers to their captors. Exchange was another form, particularly popular in the eighteenth and nineteenth centuries. Within such a system, prisoners were protected because of their value in effecting the return of soldiers previously lost to the enemy through capture.

The appropriate treatment of prisoners of war is a relatively recent topic in the history of intellectual thought. Early scholarship in philosophy on war tended to concentrate on justifying the action of the state in going to war and on a citizen's obligation to defend the state. The writings of St Augustine in the fourth and fifth centuries, from which the concept of just war theory is generally accepted as having emerged, proved pivotal to the linking of morality to military and political thought. St Augustine set out the principles that justified a state not only going to war but also established limits to a state's conduct of war. Although the rights of the individual were little alluded to by St Augustine, later scholars, as Donald Wells has pointed out, did begin to give attention to the matter. Vitoria (1485–1546), a Dominican neo-scholastic, asked whether in a just war it was lawful to kill all the guilty or to kill those who had surrendered. He concluded that a war against unbelievers allowed for their total annihilation but that a war against Christians did not. Those who entered a war in good faith were entitled to the moral protection of that faith.[1] More moderate voices began to appear in the following century. Johann Textor (1638–1701) argued that war did not convey 'any right to kill soldiers who had surrendered'.[2] Christian Wolff (1679–1754) agreed with this summation 'since one ceases to be an enemy as soon as he is in my power'.³ Emmerich Vattel (1714–1767) was similarly disposed on the question although he allowed that reprisals were permissible against enemies known to have been in grave breach of the laws of war.⁴

The rights of men surrendering in battle and their subsequent fate had clearly not been defined adequately or in any form that could be construed as representing a customary practice by the onset of the Marlborough era of warfare. The professional conduct of war, its laws and customs, began to be given higher priority by the dominant nation states in the eighteenth and nineteenth centuries. The establishment of military academies throughout Europe, Britain and America meant future officers were schooled not only in the political, strategic and tactical concepts of war but also the attendant moral and ethical considerations.

It might be argued that such thoughts were undermined by the emergence of Clausewitz's ruthless philosophy of war. Arguing that war was a rational instrument of the state and that, once engaged, it was of necessity a law unto itself he stated his case plainly:

> philanthropists may easily imagine there is a skilful method of disarming and overcoming the enemy without causing great bloodshed, and that is the proper tendency of the Art of War...it is an error that must be extirpated; for such dangerous things as War, the errors which proceed from a spirit of benevolence are the worst.⁵

While Clausewitz's philosophy was framed around the higher end of the military equation – that is, the actions of generals and statesmen – the tone of his doctrine and its stressing of the utmost use of force did not augur well for soldiers caught in bloody conflicts so conducted.

Nevertheless, the professional officers of Western nations were schooled with many of the same values and with knowledge drawn from identical or similar texts. The existence of such military schooling assisted the transmission of known customs and codes of conduct in the prosecution of war within opposition armies, particularly through the developing tradition of attachment and secondment to other armies as observers. General principles of clemency and mercy to surrendering enemy soldiers and the protection of civilian populations, even if not codified, were broadly understood by the middle of the nineteenth century. They were practised and understood as customs of war.

The specific plight and rights of the individual soldier in war did not begin to be given proper attention until midway through the nineteenth century. Henry Dunant's book *A Memory of Solferino*, in which he detailed the suffering of the wounded French, Italian and Austrian soldiers left on that northern Italian battlefield, shocked the sensibilities of European humanitarians. A special committee of concerned Swiss citizens (including Dunant) met to give thought to the protection and relief of sick and wounded soldiers. From those discussions, a wider conference was organised in Geneva in 1863, to which experts from sixteen European countries were invited. Here, the founding principles for the organisation later to become known as the Red Cross were established. The following year, at the invitation of the Swiss government, twenty-six representatives from sixteen countries ratified a treaty – the Geneva Convention – which sought to guarantee the amelioration of conditions affecting the wounded of armies in the field.[6]

While Dunant was writing his book, the United States of America had divided and plunged into fratricidal civil war. Concerned over confusion by officers and men as to how laws of war ought to be applied in time of civil war, the US government issued a manual to provide guidance on what soldiers were permitted to do. Professor Francis Lieber of Columbia University was charged with drafting the document. Appearing in 1863 under the title *General Orders 100: Instructions for the Government of Armies of the United States in the Field*, the manual was distributed to officers of both the Union and Confederate armies. A defining statement on how men should act was set down in paragraph 15:

Men who take up arms against one another in a public war do not cease on this account to be moral beings, responsible to one another and to God.[7]

Under these guidelines, men in battle were clearly expected to show due regard to their fellow man in accordance with the goodwill advocated through Christian beliefs. A further statement, contained in paragraph 68, reflected the principle of justifiable force. It stated, unequivocally, that '[u]nnecessary or revengeful destruction of life is not lawful'.[8] Killing prisoners was obviously unlawful under this direction.

The concept of 'no quarter', which had defined warfare on many occasions through the ages, was not encouraged in *General Orders 100*. It was, however, given qualified support. Paragraph 60 allowed a commander to issue such orders if attending to prisoners would encumber his command's salvation. Such an act would be interpreted as military necessity. In addition, paragraph 62 allowed no quarter in reciprocity against troops that were known to practise it.[9]

General Orders 100, or the Lieber Code as it was otherwise known, was an important document, as it provided a model from which other nations could work as well as prompting discussions on all its facets in the decades to come.[10] The successful establishment of the Red Cross and subsequent broad international acceptance of the Hague and Geneva Conventions saw the protection of the individual in war advanced significantly within the conduct of war between nations.

Prominent heads of state were drawn to the process. Czar Alexander II of Russia called a conference in St Petersburg in which he suggested the ban of an exploding bullet developed by his own country's military authorities. It proved a landmark agreement in international military relations prohibiting the use of 'projectiles under 400 grams weight'. This agreement became known as the Declaration of St Petersburg 1868. In addition, The Declaration of Brussels, made in August 1874, expressly outlawed the application of 'no quarter' as well as the 'murder' of antagonists who had surrendered at discretion.[11]

Another code with particular significance to First World War soldiers was the Hague Rules 1899, which emanated from a peace conference convened in Brussels following the suggestion of Czar Nicholas II. Building on the Declaration of St Petersburg, a ban was instituted against the use of expanding bullets such as the 'dumdum' used by British troops in the Boer War and, previously, against native populations.[12] These bullets flattened on contact with the human body and caused dreadful wounds.[13]

The Hague Rules, set down in 1899 and revised in 1907, moved towards more explicitly guaranteeing the humane treatment of prisoners and gave extensive consideration to the obligations of governments and armies in the treatment of prisoners of war. Of specific pertinence to the conduct of the individual in combat with which this book is concerned was Article 23. It stated (in part),

> In addition to the prohibitions provided by special Conventions, it is especially forbidden –
> To employ poison or poisoned weapons;
> To kill or wound treacherously individuals belonging to the hostile nation or army;
> To kill or wound an enemy who, having laid down his arms, or having no longer means of defence, has surrendered at discretion;
> To declare that no quarter will be given;
> To employ arms, projectiles, or material calculated to cause unnecessary suffering;
> To make improper use of a flag of truce, of the national flag or the military insignia and uniform of the enemy, as well as the distinctive badges of the Geneva Convention.[14]

While not all the Great Powers were signatories to the revised version, the failure of these nations to ratify it did not necessarily mean they rejected the terms and conditions outright or that they would not abide by the spirit of the laws. Where agreement was not reached by contracting parties, the 1899 rules stood. Britain, in fact, did incorporate the Hague Convention in its *Manual of Military Law* published in 1914 and 1916. Chapter XIV, paragraph 50, reiterated that the act of killing prisoners who had laid down their arms was forbidden. Furthermore, the British manual stated in the next paragraph (51),

> This prohibition is clear and distinct; there is no question of the moment up to which acts of violence may be continued without disentitling the enemy to being ultimately admitted to the benefit of quarter. War is for the purpose of overcoming armed resistance, and no vengeance can be taken because an individual has done his duty to the last but escaped injury.[15]

Understanding of a surrendered enemy's rights was unequivocal. So, too, was the undertaking in the next paragraph (52) that '[c]are must therefore be taken that all ranks are acquainted with the laws of war and that they endeavour to observe them'.[16]

As members of the British Army conversant with the *Manual of Military Law*, there can be no doubt that Australian officers were aware of their obligations in this respect. Moreover, given the large portion of officers drawn from the legal fraternity, there exist few reasons to believe that Australian officers did not comprehend their responsibilities towards ensuring the prevention of such treachery.

The degree to which the rank and file understood their responsibilities is perhaps less certain. Nevertheless, it was the responsibility of officers to instruct them in such matters if they did not already know. An important aspect of the *Manual of Military Law* was contained in paragraph 433. It required combatants to obey all commands issued by a superior officer. This, as Joanna Bourke points out, ran counter to the prevailing custom that soldiers were only compelled to obey 'lawful orders'. The United States army also adopted a similar view and its 1914 edition of the *Rules of Land Warfare* absolved individuals of any blame when acting under orders of their commanders.[17]

The British Army did endeavour to make these rules understood. Treatment of enemy prisoners was one of the many topics taught to officers and NCOs in the schools of instruction behind the lines during the war. Captain J.H. Honeysett thought it an 'irony of fate' that he had delivered a lecture at the 4th Australian Divisional School on the treatment of enemy prisoners of war a few weeks prior to his capture at Bullecourt.[18] Circulars, too, were distributed. These included details on how to conduct prisoners to the rear with specific instructions on what could and could not be taken from them.[19]

Of particular interest was a circular issued and titled 'The Soldiers' Don'ts of International Law'.[20] This document was clearly designed as a ready reckoner for soldiers to know theirs and their enemy's rights in battle. It concluded with commendable legal and Christian intent: 'DON'T go beyond your rights, and DO as you would be done by.' A reading of the list reveals some odd inconsistencies of intent and admiration. With quirky British grace it suggested, 'DON'T shoot a spy off hand; he is doing a very plucky thing, and deserves a trial…'

21

It preceded this with a stern and unsympathetic warning: 'DON'T rub or file your bullets; if you are caught with such bullets on you, you will be shot, and serve you right.' Yet in regard to the act of killing surrendering soldiers it was ambivalent. What interpretation would a soldier put on the advice 'DON'T kill a man who has thrown his arms down as a sign that he has ceased to resist' when it was followed by 'DON'T be heartbroken if you kill such a one by mistake – it is his fault for having resisted up till too late'?

Without doubt, Australian soldiers in the First World War were aware of the fundamental rights of the individual in battle. The degree to which they derived this from their own Christian-based morality, through informed opinion about the International debates on the issue or from the army's own instruction, is uncertain. Generally speaking, it is difficult to see how they cannot have had some understanding of how to act towards the surrendering or captured enemy given the British Army's obvious – even if ambiguous – commitment to upholding International law.

Translating these understandings from the manuals and applying them under the duress of combat was, however, a process tinged with uncertainty. Such application of the laws (as they were understood) would vary with the emotional intelligence of the individual as well as the discipline and leadership within the units to which soldiers belonged. It is apparent that some Australian officers harboured an uncompromising attitude towards the enemy from the outset that was clearly communicated to their soldiers. For example, one can only surmise as to what attitudes were fomenting within the Victorian raised 22nd Battalion prior to its arrival at the Western Front. At its first battalion parade, the unit was addressed by Colonel Crouch, who announced 'Wipe out the bloody Germans' as the regimental motto. Despite criticisms from prominent clerics and some newspaper discussion, the motto stuck in abbreviated form – W.O.T.B.G – and formed part of a chorus in the regimental song.[21] How widespread this sentiment was forms part of the discussion of the following chapters.

Two

Gallipoli – 'the Australian when he fights, fights all in'

The fact that Australian soldiers did sometimes kill their prisoners or refuse to take prisoners has generally been accommodated within robust assertions of masculinity contained within Australia's First World War story. The 'digger' was a fighter not a soldier. Hard-nosed in his prosecution of war but a thoroughly likeable and compassionate chap once the gloves were off. This view certainly underpinned C.E.W. Bean's attitude throughout his volumes of the official histories. To Bean's credit, at no stage did he attempt to deny Australian involvement in acts that might be considered deplorable. He did, however, often seek to qualify if not justify those that came to his notice.

Writing prior to the publication of the official histories, General Sir John Monash, as we have seen, offered a contrary view. Not surprisingly, given their importance to Monash's reputation, his description of the Australian soldier as 'sportsmen' mirrored Bean's later virtuous renderings. Like Monash, Bean shared an equally strong desire to uphold the reputation of the Australian soldier, though he was undoubtedly more candid than Australia's most famous general on the subject. Yet the writings of both men, and Bean particularly, were highly influential in shaping the public's opinion on such matters. For that reason alone, a chronological examination of Bean's accounts (in this chapter and the next) of such incidents is essential to determining his attitude to such behaviour. It also provides us with an overview of the variations in warfare in which the Australians were involved. This is important, as the various phases of the war and tactics used definitely influenced the decision-making process of soldiers in determining whether to kill or spare the enemy.

Naturally, it was Gallipoli that provided the context for Bean's first engagement with the treatment of enemy prisoners. In writing the 'Story of Anzac' Bean was quick to confront the issue and portray the Australian soldier in the best possible light. He stated that the men had entered the battle with the belief that the Turks were prone to mutilating and killing the wounded and prisoners. According to Bean, officers who had previous experience with the Kurds and ill-disciplined Turkish troops had provided the information. So armed, the men manifested a hatred towards the enemy.[1]

This was fanned by a willingness to accept racial stereotypes that depicted the Turks as unchristian and bestial. *The Bulletin*, for example, in one report referred to the Turks as 'ignorant heathens'.[2] Portrayed in this way, their alleged barbarity was more easily understood. A further consequence was that, being non-Christian, their status as foes worthy of protection under the rules of war may have been undermined in the eyes of Allied troops.

Preferring to project the honourable nature of Australian soldiers, Bean cited the example of a Turk captured by two men of the 10th Battalion as they scrambled up the slopes above North Beach at Ari Burnu on the day of the landing. The pair of West Australians resisted the recommendations of their mates to 'Shoot the bastard!', allowing Bean to declare, 'as in every battle he fought, the Australian soldier was more humane in his deeds than in his words. The Turk was sent down to the beach in charge of a wounded man.'[3]

Such altruism, if widely practised, was all the more magnanimous given the belief held by many Australian soldiers during the first few days and subsequent weeks on Anzac that the Turks mutilated prisoners. The death of Sergeant E.R. Larkin, a member of the 1st Battalion and formerly of the New South Wales Legislative Assembly, killed during the fighting upon 400 Plateau on the first day, was offered as proof of the enemy's barbaric inclination. Retreating Australians brought back reports that his body had been badly mutilated. When Larkin's body was recovered during the armistice of 24 May, no evidence of deliberate mutilation was discovered. He had been killed by machine-gun fire, the mangled state of his body a testament to the destructive capacity of that weapon upon the human form.[4]

The Larkin incident demonstrated how quickly trench rumour could take root. Its influence in shaping behaviour towards the enemy must necessarily be considered. Taken singularly, the truth of Larkin's demise did not disprove or dilute the general belief in Turkish brutality. It would seem, also, that the Turks were conscious of allaying such fears. A note thrown into the Australian trenches read, in part, 'Be convinced that everybody of you who has been taken prisoner will be treated just as well as international law commands'.[5] The Turks well understood the benefit of an enemy not afraid to surrender, as opposed to one predisposed to fighting to the death.

How genuinely the Turks held to such a view is arguable. The story of Corporal George Kerr, 14th Battalion, who was captured near Hill 971, provides a disquieting awareness of what the fate of many Australian soldiers cut off or wounded and lying beyond salvation was likely to have been. The young corporal was part of a group that chose to surrender. His injured commanding lieutenant was shot after laying down his arms. Kerr, himself wounded, lay helplessly as his comrades were bayoneted and bludgeoned to death. Fortunately, one of the Turks showed restraint, fashioned a staff from a branch, and sent Kerr to the rear and captivity.[6]

Bean was critical of the Turkish attitude and behaviour towards Australians caught under similar circumstances. He vented his frustration over the fate of the remnants of the Australian line surrounded on Pine Ridge after the collapse of that position on the afternoon of 25 April 1915. A Turk claimed (during the 24 May armistice) that they had been forced to kill the Australians because they had feigned death and then fired upon the Turks as they passed.[7] Bean dismissed this claim as 'transparent and insufficient', pointing to the fact that none of the Australians reported as wounded on the ridge were ever made a prisoner of war.[8]

If Bean was crying foul in this regard, he might well be accused of slight hypocrisy for his uncritical presentation of an incident involving Major I. Jackson's company of the 9th Battalion as it pushed inland over Little Ari Burnu near Hell's Spit on the first morning at Gallipoli. Consider the official historian's account:

A desultory rifle fire was coming from the slopes ahead of it. As the company moved down the back of Little Ari Burnu into the valley, it found a small stone hut, in which were half a dozen Turks and a small fire with a pot of coffee on it. The Turks were bayoneted.[9]

Had these been the Turks issuing the desultory fire Bean mentioned? His description suggests not. The slopes ahead of Jackson's company, which was bearing south-eastward, were probably those of McCay's Hill or the Razorback. Bean does not mention any severe fighting. A desultory fire was hardly evidence, even if it emanated from the six Turks, of a determined resistance. The brewing coffee and the fact that the Queenslanders 'found' the Turks suggests an element of surprise. There is no suggestion that the Turks violently resisted the Australian arrival. If Jackson's men were close enough to bayonet the Turks, why were they not taken prisoner? An escort or even two could surely have been detached from a full half company.

The absence of comment in this instance is probably telling. Bean did not want to judge the officers or men. The compassion he had lauded only a few pages earlier was clearly compromised if the Australians had acted ruthlessly in despatching men who were clearly no threat. Yet his commitment to maintaining a true and accurate historical record, and his journalistic integrity, worked against excluding the event altogether.

Explanation for why the Australians showed no mercy in this instance, as well as Bean's unease on the subject, are evident in the diaries he kept. Four days after the landing, Bean recorded that he had been told by Australians and New Zealanders 'that they had orders from their subordinate officers in some cases to take no prisoners, in the first rush at any rate, and whilst things were bad.' He added, 'I don't believe this either, though it may be true.'[10]

Bean did not want to believe that such orders had been issued, even though he conceded the possibility. As part of the 3rd Brigade, Jackson's men were in the 'first rush' but things were hardly 'bad' for them at the time. Any claims to military necessity were thin indeed. In those early hours of 25 April 1915, it would seem that Major Jackson had invoked a policy of no quarter or tacitly accepted its implementation. The Australians, as the Turks did on Pine Ridge hours later, had clearly contravened the rules of war as laid down in Article 23 of the Hague Convention and British military manuals.

Although Bean's disapproval at such a possibility was evident, it sat incongruously against his celebration of the spirit of the Australian soldier. In the same entry, he made comparison of the Australian soldier with his New Zealand counterpart. He quoted an Australian soldier as saying, 'Kind hearted beggars, the N. Zealanders a Turk snipes them and then they catch the beggar and take him by the hand and lead him down to the beach...'[11] The imputation was clear. The Australians would have shown no such clemency. Bean took the opportunity to point out a fundamental difference in national character as he saw it: 'undoubtedly the N.Z. fights more with his gloves on than the Australian: the Australian when he fights, fights all in.'[12]

Later, when describing the capture of seventeen Turks at Quinn's Post, Bean reasserted the kinder aspects of Australian behaviour while still maintaining the moral high ground:

> The wretched survivors were terror-stricken, apprehending the fate too often reserved for any wounded enemy who fell into their hands. But the waiting Australians slapped them on the back and offered them cigarettes as they marched down the hill.[13]

The Turks were also capable of displaying similar benevolence towards their prisoners, as Private D.B. Creedon's account reveals. He was pleasantly surprised to find himself alive after he had been wounded and fallen asleep and subsequently captured by three Turks. He had not thought for a moment that they would take him prisoner. He was treated kindly throughout his journey from the line, offered cigarettes by passing Turkish soldiers, fed and given medical attention. Later treatment was considerably less accommodating and he would die in captivity. However, in those first hours after capture, his main grievance was not the treatment by his guards but rather what he regarded as the craven behaviour of his commanding officer, Lieutenant J—, who repeatedly asked for mercy for himself and his men.[14]

The benevolent Australian attitude was certainly preferred by Bean, and feeds into the general mythology that Australian attitudes to their enemy became more respectful after the display of bravery and slaughter of Turkish troops in the massed attacks on 19 May. Again, Bean's diaries prove more illuminating than his official histories in providing contrary evidence of the Australian character. When, during the August offensive, a compound for Turkish prisoners was erected near his dugout, Bean witnessed several instances of provocation by the Australians in regard to their prisoners. The worst (and one repeated) was the pouring of kerosene uncomfortably close by the compound. This was then lit, much to the glee of the Australian and British crowd, who laughed as the helpless Turks 'stampeded' from the perceived danger. Bean wondered why 'someone hadn't the decency to hit the man who did it straight in the face... The treatment of these prisoners makes you blush for your own side.'[15] For many, such actions were written off as examples of high jinks. Yet they were clearly an abrogation of those prisoners' rights to be treated in a humane manner. Part of the problem in this instance, according to Bean, was the poor selection of Indian guards, who proved incapable of keeping the Australians away.[16]

It must be said that Australian mistreatment of Turkish prisoners or of the more serious crime of their murder is not much in evidence. Bean was most likely correct in differentiating between Australian braggadoccio on the matter and their actions, although the degree to which incidents were not recorded remains problematic.

One evident truth was that both sides in the opening weeks of the campaign were ignorant of the other. Soldiers of both the Ottoman and British Empires feared they would be murdered if they fell into the hands of their enemy, as was noted in one account of the campaign:

> Incidentally, I may say, prisoners all believed they were going to be killed. I remember Major Martyn telling me how one party, on coming through a communication trench to our lines, had tried to kiss his hands in gratitude at being spared.[17]

For both sides, the static nature of the Gallipoli campaign meant that, other than the landing, the 19 May Turkish attack and the August offensive, there were few opportunities where prisoners could be taken. Overall, a total of 232 Australians were captured by the Turks during the First World War. Only a third of these represented soldiers captured at Gallipoli. Of these, approximately twenty-five per cent died in captivity.[18]

Three

'Kill every bloody German you see, we don't want any prisoners, and God bless you'

The Western Front, where 3,850 Australians were captured, provided far greater opportunity to take prisoners and offers a greater range of experience in which to examine the questions pertaining to appropriate treatment at the moment of and following a soldier's capitulation.[1] The larger-scale battles in France and Belgium, regular trench raids and brief moments of open warfare all provided opportunities in which the enemy lines or portions of it were breached or overrun. It also offered engagement with a different enemy. If the Turk had been seriously underestimated as a foe, and irrespective of whether Australian soldiers abandoned Gallipoli with a newfound respect for him or not, Turkey was still considered of secondary importance and not the real enemy.

From the outbreak of the war and throughout the Gallipoli campaign, the bestial Hun had become a feature of Australian propaganda. The Australian public, prospective volunteers and the soldiers already enlisted received a steady diet of anti-German literature. In 1917, the Director General of Recruiting in Victoria issued a booklet titled *German Atrocities* that catalogued a series of alleged barbarities enacted by German troops for the public's edification.[2] How effective this was in shaping perceptions towards the enemy is difficult to know. A cursory glance of Australian soldiers' diaries and letters reveal extensive use of the less flattering pseudonyms of 'Hun' and 'Squarehead' in preference to the more amiable 'Fritz' and 'Jerry'. Such word usage may be indicative of a manifest hatred but whether it was likely to be translated into acts of intolerance or barbarity on the battlefield is largely immeasurable.

Like the men of 1915, those arriving in France in 1916 had little conception of the nature of the war they were entering or of the enemy they were to confront. It is possible that they entered the line in a heightened state of combativeness, intent on proving themselves and upholding a reputation of the Australian soldier as a fearsome warrior which was already in vogue. If so, they may have been predisposed to adopt an uncompromising attitude against the 'real' enemy.

When the Australians arrived in France, they were allocated a quiet sector near Armentières known as the 'Nursery' to acclimatise to the conditions of trench warfare. The period of acclimatisation gave way to a general undertaking of trench raiding as Douglas Haig began preparations for his Somme offensive to relieve pressure on the French at Verdun.

The trench raid was designed as a lightning strike against the enemy, with a variety of purposes in mind. It was considered a means of keeping one's own troops in fine fighting fettle while keeping the enemy on edge. It was a means by which opposing troops could be identified through killing, wounding or capture. Sometimes the raids were retaliatory, a reaction to a recent enemy incursion and a means by which the ledger could be squared. The raid, too, was conducted with the brutal intent of doing as much damage to the enemy in as short a period of time as possible.

Killing the enemy had become an object of the trench raid. First Brigade orders to raiding parties of the 2nd and 3rd Battalions in October 1916 made no attempt to disguise the fact. The object of the raid was

(a.) To take prisoners
(b.) To kill enemy
(c.) To obtain information
(d.) To capture war material
(e.) To destroy works and dug-outs.[3]

It is important to understand that the trench raid was a tactic that arose from the peculiarities of the extensive trench warfare confronting generals and their men during the First World War. When the Hague Rules of 1899 and 1907 were drafted, its provisions were undoubtedly based upon the more open nature of battle as it was conceived and fought previously. The trench raid, in its conception, disregarded fundamental guidelines expressed in Article 23 of the Hague Rules. The nature of the trench raid itself also made it difficult for even the most virtuous soldiers to maintain the level of humanity that international law intended. The risky, nerve-racking and brutal nature of raids and patrols meant they were not missions necessarily sought by the men. Volunteers were called for, often with the enticement of a concession of extra rest for the participants.[4]

Paramount to a raid's success and raider's survival was the ability to escape unharmed back to friendly lines before enemy counterattacks and counter-bombardments could be brought to bear. The nature of the raid immediately compromised the rights of surrendering soldiers. An attacking soldier might reasonably argue that to be encumbered with prisoners was to compromise his own safety. Better, then, to take none. The phrase and argument invoked to defend such action was that of military necessity.

A further compromising aspect was the development of weapons designed particularly for use in close-quarter fighting. A variety of clubs and edged weapons were designed to contribute to the destruction of the enemy, and some, no doubt, with the intent of inspiring blood lust in the heart and mind of the bearer. Alternatively, the use of clubs might also be regarded as an indication of men's natural aversion to using edged weapons in close combat.[5]

Blood lust featured early in Bean's description of trench raiding in France. He argued that a 'primitive bloodthirstiness' took possession of most men particularly in close-quarter fighting. Bean accepted its presence as inevitable in both armies because the men were 'wrought up by the strain to an intense desire to strike' with orders 'to inflict as much loss as possible', and their duty required that 'they spend the few allotted minutes in striking at everything around them, killing, wounding, or capturing'. As a consequence, he admitted that the details did not make pleasant reading and cited the case of a German sergeant who was hauled from a dugout and shot several times after showing plucky resistance. The German sergeant was described as sinking helplessly to the ground, though it is not stated whether he was dead or not.⁶ The 'brave man' was later 'brained by the knobkerry of some soldier whose lust for blood was not yet satisfied'.⁷

Bean was not condoning such behaviour. He obviously thought the braining of the sergeant was an insulting final indignity administered to a 'brave' and 'plucky' man. Yet he reconciled his disappointment against the argument that such an act was 'inseparable from the exercise of the primitive instincts'.⁸ Should we accept such a premise? Or is it incompatible with understanding man as a rational and moral being? Studies of US soldiers in the Second World War show that, far from possessing barbaric primitive instincts for killing, the majority of soldiers possess an instinctive resistance to killing. As writers such as Grossman and Bourke have shown, it was this very resistance that armies are committed to breaking down through propaganda and training.

There are undoubtedly psychological and physiological factors that contribute to man's inability to think and act rationally on occasion. Men engaging in combat, anxious, overwrought and fearful of losing their own lives represent one group most definitely operating at the extreme end of human behaviour. That concession must be made generally. However, it should not provide any blanket approval or apology for excessive blood lust in combat. In the example of the brave German sergeant, Bean points out that his three comrades who subsequently surrendered were 'apparently' spared.⁹ The use of 'apparently' is not convincing but let us assume the best. Here, then, in the acceptance of the Germans' surrender, we see the raiders making a rational decision, acting in a compassionate manner and observing the rules of war. Their ability to do this undermines carte blanche acceptance of engaging in a killing spree against garrisons who, Bean concedes, were 'thoroughly cowed' by the supporting bombardment. Such men clearly represented no threat, were unlikely to offer resistance and, given such passivity, had every right to be given the opportunity to surrender and be made prisoners of war.

The dynamics of the trench raid naturally created problems of identification as to those who posed a threat and those who did not. Germans appearing suddenly around corners, even if themselves unaware of the raid in progress and even if unarmed, were likely to be shot down, bombed or bayoneted. To survive, attacking soldiers had to assume that all those who confronted them were hostile in intent. It would be unreasonable to expect soldiers to operate on any other premise. It was not unreasonable, and indeed Australian soldiers proved its possibility time and again, to arrive at a point during the raid that did allow reasonable assessments to be made about an opponent's intent and to capture rather than kill.

Limited time allotted to raiders also circumscribed the men's ability to ponder such inexactitudes. Only seven minutes were to be spent in the enemy trenches for the first Australian raid on the German line on 6 June 1916 by a combined party of the 26th and 28th Battalions. Led by Captain Maitland Foss, a West Australian farmer, it proved totally successful. The previous example of the 'plucky' German sergeant is drawn from it. This raid also revealed other aspects inherent to the life and death issues confronting attackers and defenders. Language was one. Bean recorded two captured Germans being killed because of their failure to respond instantly to 'some order'.[10] Had the Germans understood the order? Possibly not, and the haste and anxiety that marked the parameters for the Australian presence in the German trenches without doubt diminished the attackers' capacity for patience and tolerance. German officers appeared to be better skilled in speaking English than their Australian and British counterparts at speaking German. It is likely that Australian soldiers tended to benefit more from this than did Germans captured by non-German-speaking Australians.

A second factor that seemed to influence the choice of life and death was the youthfulness of the enemy soldiers. Those described or regarded as boys often evoked a measure of compassion in the heart of the attacker. A sense of inappropriateness of a 'man' killing a 'boy' seemed to exist. Perhaps it compromised the sense of a 'fair go' that Australian soldiers were said to harbour. Captain Foss, on entering a dugout and firing into an empty bundle of blankets, discovered a 'boy' with his hands up. Commendably, the captain chose to haul the lad out and throw him over the parapet to his waiting scouts rather than end a young life.[11]

Much as men hardened themselves to the idea of killing, they were themselves susceptible to the guilt it could bring. For raiders, the discovery of letters, photographs, delicacies and associated trinkets that linked their opponents with the comforts and joys of civilian life created disquiet in their minds. Such things reminded men of the frailty of their own connections with home. It was something Bean fully understood.[12]

Raiding increased in the latter part of June and early July of 1916 as British preparations for the Somme offensive intensified. Bean recorded a number of the Australian and New Zealand raids in an extensive chart that read something like a scoreboard detailing comparative casualties and incidents of note.[13] Of particular interest is Bean's notation in regard to a raid by the 3rd NZ Infantry Brigade. Conducted on the night of 25–26 June 1916, a large number of Germans, many whom offered 'little resistance', were shot down and bombed as the raiders undertook a fifteen-minute operation of destruction. In this instance, orders had been issued which limited to three the amount of prisoners to be taken. Nine were listed as captured, a measure of limited compassion perhaps. Bean acknowledged that such orders, written or verbal, contradicted the spirit of the rules of war but argued that it was not the general practice of British, New Zealand or Australian commanders to issue them.[14]

It was the major battles rather than the raids for which the rules governing engagement with the enemy were fashioned. And it was in the large battles that large numbers of prisoners were captured. Fate and a considerable dollop of enthusiasm mixed with inexperience decreed that the first major battle in which the Australians participated on the Western Front would prove an unmitigated disaster for the AIF. On the night and morning of 19–20 July, the 5th Australian Division suffered a total of 5,533 casualties during the Battle of Fromelles. Over 400 Australians were captured.[15]

The circumstances of the Australian failure at Fromelles placed the men in an extremely compromising situation. Having gone forward, they became trapped in and between the German main line and their own. The German counter-bombardment and an enfilading fire from the flanks meant that the Australians who had breached the German defences had to lie between the lines largely unsupported and await the inevitable German counterattack. Under such circumstances, their options were limited. They could try and retreat immediately or they could hang on and defend until all ammunition was expended and then endeavour to get back. Initially, the option most favoured was to hang on and await support. As the night wore on into morning, it became increasingly obvious to those who had survived that their fate was ultimately capture or death.

In such a situation, men so entrapped could minimise their chances of being killed by becoming passive and presenting a non-threatening attitude to the enemy or fleeing. When large numbers of men have been captured, it is certain that a moment is reached, almost collectively, in which they forfeit their aggressive instincts and opt for survival. Reversion to such a pragmatic and natural impulse is hardly surprising. Indeed, Bean acknowledged its grip upon the mind of Australian soldiers when he described elements of the 53rd Battalion continuing to stream towards the rear. Officers were unable to stem the tide, managing to rally only a 'few badly shaken men'.[16]

The most obvious act by which a soldier could demonstrate his passiveness when confronted by an enemy was to raise his arms above his head. It was also a universally understood sign. When Captain C. Mills found himself surrounded, his German counterpart jumped into the trench and asked, 'Why did you not put up your hands, officer? Come with me.'[17]

For groups and individuals no longer capable of resistance either because they were incapacitated, out of ammunition or had decided that further resistance was futile, the raising of a white flag or something similar was generally and universally recognised. At Fromelles, isolated groups opted for this reasonable course.[18] The advantage of such a visible sign was that it communicated to the enemy at distance one's desire to surrender. By so doing, the less certain responses that visited men during battle could be minimised. It allowed the enemy time to digest the fact that the threat to them had been removed or considerably diminished, a reaction that might – in turn – cause them to act in a reasonable manner.

Given the heavy casualties at Fromelles and given the number of prisoners lost, it was not surprising that tired and dispirited soldiers were receptive to stories that the Germans had shot men after surrender. Bean resisted the temptation and cited the example of Lance-corporal T. Driscoll of the 8th Machine-gun Battalion. Driscoll had lain wounded in no-man's land all day before being brought in by four Bavarians who struggled through mud and wire under machine-gun fire to rescue him.[19]

The succour of the wounded had been the inspiration for Henri Dunant's campaign to establish internationally recognised conventions in war. At Fromelles, a situation presented itself in which hundreds of Australian wounded were left unattended between the opposing lines. Their cries and the sight of their physical discomfort pained and demoralised those forced to endure it. Some risked life and limb to bring relief to them and temper the suffering.

Private W. Miles, an Englishman, ex-sailor and veteran of the South African War and now member of the 29th Australian Infantry Battalion, was one of these men. Miles had ventured into no-man's land in search of his company officer Captain Mortimer. A German officer beckoned to him and suggested that, if he returned with an officer, a parliamentaire might be arranged in which the wounded could be collected. Miles did so and returned with Major A.W. Murdoch who asked if an informal truce might be arranged. After telephoning for further instructions, the German officer advised that his headquarters agreed to the proposal provided that German stretcher-bearers work one side and make prisoner those they collected and the Australian rescue those in their designated zone. It was a fair proposal and mirrored that undertaken with the Turks at Anzac on 24 May 1915.

The proposal was telephoned through to divisional headquarters. In the interim, an informal truce was entered into. Australians collected their wounded while the Germans repaired their trenches. The respite was short-lived, as the 5th Division commander, General J.W. McCay, declined the humane offer. Pressing upon his mind was a GHQ directive not to engage in any negotiation with the enemy. In recording this, Bean inclined to the view that the Australian army and nation would have leaned towards acceptance of the truce as an expression of 'the principles of humanity and chivalry, for which the Allies generally stood'.[20] He did not blame McCay, arguing that a divisional commander's rigid adherence to orders from the commander-in-chief was understandable. Fear that the enemy would gain morally and through propaganda played a part in such philosophy.

When all was said and done, however, the only group that could have gained from a truce was the many wounded Australians. A more courageous commander and one more attuned to his men's needs might have acted differently but McCay, through his inaction, proved himself not to be that man.

The fate of soldiers caught in the first rush of an attacking enemy was subject to great uncertainty. Little time was available to reach consensus on whether to surrender or resist. Their own comrades sometimes undid the expected security of surrender. Bean recorded an incident at Pozières where four Germans 'wished' to surrender but 'were immediately killed' when a fifth 'bravely' threw a bomb.[21] For Bean, it appears that this act of bravery (or foolhardiness) was enough to sanction the killing of the other four. How, one might reasonably ask, was it not possible for the Australian or Australians then present to discern between one combative German and four who were obviously making clear their intentions to surrender?

Mention has already been made of the process of 'ratting' at Pozières. As was suggested, Bean's official acceptance of it belies his personal principles in regard to fair and proper treatment towards prisoners. An incident in which a German was shot dead after firing three rounds at an Australian patrol leader, Lieutenant Laing, led Bean to state, '[I]t is idle for men so caught to expect mercy.'[22] One can only concur that the 12th Battalion soldier who shot the German did the right thing in defending Laing. However, the official historian's account of Laing's subsequent action is notably lacking in critical comment.

Laing wrote that one German in a wireless dugout attempted to surrender when he found the Australians suddenly on top of him. One of the soldiers was inclined to capture the surrendering German and called for him to come out. On hearing this, Laing rushed back and told the chap to shoot the swine or he would. The soldier complied.[23] This was leadership of the basest kind.

The German – in the estimations of Laing, and presumably the official historian, given his lack of disapproval – may not have deserved mercy but he was entitled to it under the rules of war. The reason advanced for the Australian intolerance was that these Germans were occupying the ground from which snipers had fired. Yet the Australians' application of no quarter was clearly inconsistent and indiscriminate, given the fact that the patrol killed six and captured eighteen.[24]

Another point worthy of consideration is that Bean always accepted the notion that men who fought until their ammunition was expended were acting bravely and appropriately. He made a fine distinction between such brave hearts and those who ceased firing at the last moment to surrender. Those men could not expect mercy from their attackers, who had sustained casualties and were primed to exact some retribution. But where lies the distinction for an attacking force to assess whether their enemy has run out of ammunition or are surrendering at the last minute? For example, would Bean have been accepting of a situation in which the Germans, arguing their case along his lines, decided to show no mercy to men of the 48th Battalion whose bomb supply ran short and surrendered upon the enemy closing in?[25] One suspects he would have invoked the same sense of outrage that he had reserved for the Turks' actions on Pine Ridge cited earlier.

When attacking trenches, the standard practice of the opposing armies on the Western Front was to roll bombs into dugouts rather than risk danger entering them. Sentries were placed at the entrance to capture or kill any survivors who opted to surrender. A phosphorus bomb was often thrown in afterwards to encourage recalcitrants to emerge, though it was a particularly callous act to inflict upon wounded men trapped in the chambers. Often, a summons to surrender would be issued before such drastic action was commenced. For men trapped in dugouts, surrender, despite its uncertainty, was the more expedient measure.

Such tactics were less effective when attacking enemy outposts, as the open warfare that accompanied the German withdrawal in early 1917 proved. Depending on their inclination, defenders of outposts could resist and instigate a bomb fight or a fire-fight in which the attackers might be driven off or allow time for themselves to extricate themselves.

The cut and thrust of the actions between the Australian and German patrols detailed in Bean's fourth volume makes interesting reading. It is apparent that, although the nature of the combat was more open than the major battles and trench raids, some of the same confusion existed. During an attack along Sunray Trench, a group of bewildered Germans appeared to want to surrender to the advancing 29th Battalion. Lieutenant Whitelaw went forward to call them in but was fired on by others within the party. This was rightly seen as an act of treachery and the Victorians shot down the party. It is difficult under such circumstances to believe they should have acted differently after making overtures for their opponents' surrender. In view of the conflicting German intent, the distance between the two groups and the obvious confusion and danger that manifested itself as a result, the Victorians' actions were probably reasonable.[26]

The safety of prisoners who survived the first contact with their captors was not immediately assured. They still had to be ushered to safety. At Noreuil, upwards of 100 Australians were captured. Between ten and twenty of these men were shot down by Australian machine-guns after being mistaken for Germans making towards the rear.[27] Regrettable as this was, it was an understandable consequence of war. The German escorts who would have been accompanying the prisoners would have identified the group as hostile in the minds of the Australian machine-gunners. Of course, the possibility that the Australians were deliberately shot down by their comrades must be countenanced. Bean recorded an incident at Bullecourt of an officer of the 48th (West Australian) Battalion ordering his men to fire on some of the 46th (Victorian) Battalion who he believed had surrendered too easily.[28]

Prisoners were, at times, used to assist the wounded back or to carry stretchers. This was permissible under the rules of war, though they could not be sent back towards the front to repeat the work. The use of captured men to carry ammunition, as some Germans were made to do at Bullecourt, was in direct contradiction of those laws.[29]

The battles of mid-1917 heralded a new German defence system formulated around the establishment of a series of pillboxes in the defensive perimeter. This new system had a direct impact on the behaviour of attacking soldiers towards the garrisons that led to numerous incidents in which surrendering defenders had to negotiate the wrath of their captors. The anger stemmed from the attackers having to advance under fire against these positions, take casualties and then accept the surrender of the garrison. Many men thirsted for revenge and wished to exact some form of payback. Yet no quarter was prohibited. Men and officers, particularly, knew this. Under such circumstances, the behaviour and example of officers was paramount to the safe passage of the garrisons or strong points such as farmhouses and other defended buildings.

The action of an unnamed Australian officer at Messines provides a stirring example of leadership. The officer approached a building from which a red-cross flag fluttered and beckoned for those within to surrender. At this point, the officer was shot in the shoulder from elsewhere. According to Bean, the Australian soldiers were incensed, thinking the shot had come from that building, and 'would have killed every man' but for the officer, who in 'much pain, stood in their way… to allow 30 unwounded Germans to troop out and move off unhurt as prisoners of war'.[30]

It was the actions that centred on the pillboxes or blockhouses that proved the most contentious examples in assessing Australian behaviour. During the Menin Road fighting, a party of the 20th Battalion was involved in an incident which saw an Australian Lewis-gunner shoot down a number of surrendering Germans. The Germans were emerging from a pillbox and as the first German appeared another fired between his legs, wounding a sergeant of the 20th Battalion. To this, the Lewis-gunner shouted 'Get out of the way, sergeant, I'll see to the bastards' and fired three or four bursts into the entrance killing and wounding most of those inside. Here, the action of one German, who Bean described as 'brave', compromised the position of the rest or 'weaker spirits' as Bean termed them and was symptomatic of the confusion in so many such fights which proved fatal to the garrison.[31] One suspects Bean's delineation of the surrendering Germans as 'weaker spirits' to be a deliberate means of deflecting sympathy for men he considered unworthy. Nevertheless, the Lewis-gunner's response might be regarded as something of an over-reaction. A single burst might have been enough to ensure no further resistance rather than indulging in a wholesale slaughter. Yet for a soldier primed to kill, with his blood up, and inflamed by the enemy's response, can we reasonably ask for such rational discernment? Here may be a recognisable example of Bean's 'heat of battle' argument.

Another facet of fighting, and one implied in many Australian accounts as a cowardly act undeserving of any subsequent merciful treatment, was the practise of firing machine-guns until the last moment and then surrendering. Australians, too, in all likelihood fought in this way. Not surprisingly, some Germans adopted the Australian point of view, as an incident involving Private C.H. Kennedy reveals. Kennedy, who was lying wounded after 'having inflicted fully 40 casualties on the Germans with our machine-gun before they got into the shelter of the sunken road' was saved from a vengeful lunging German bayonet by an officer who spoke perfect English.[32]

It was clear, however, that even as late as 1918, despite the issue of manuals and memorandums to the contrary, Australian soldiers were still being instructed to flagrantly disregard the rules of war. Prior to an attack at Villers-Bretonneux, company officers issued orders that, according to Captain 'Billy' Harburn, 51st Battalion, ended with the exhortation 'Kill every bloody German you see, we don't want any prisoners, and God bless you.'[33]

Harburn certainly showed himself to be a devout follower of those instructions. When confronted by an undisclosed number of the enemy who put their hands up in surrender, Harburn gave the order 'No prisoners'. His defence afterwards was that he did not know what to do with them.[34] Even allowing for the fact that his company was 'much weakened', his was a flimsy and shallow excuse for such a murderous act. Finding oneself in straitened circumstances did not have to mean a death sentence under military necessity for enemy prisoners. A party of 21st Battalion ensnared at Mouquet Farm 'made strenuous efforts' to reach the sanctuary of their own lines while bringing along three captured Germans, though it must be acknowledged that the statement from which that incident is drawn did not say what finally happened to the Germans.[35]

The war provided countless examples of single soldiers escorting larger bodies of prisoners to the rear and of prisoners being sent back unescorted. Harburn's first action is brought into even starker relief when, soon after, his men, after an unexpected clash with the enemy, captured sixty Germans and sent them to the rear.[36] It is further eroded by the fact that two of Harburn's men captured forty enemy soldiers shortly afterward.[37] It is difficult, from reading Bean's account, to interpret Harburn's situation as so critical as to not allow prisoners to have been taken in the first instance.

Another incident at Villers-Bretonneux passed with equal muteness from the official historian. A patrol led by Lieutenant Simpson, 60th Battalion, captured a German post but was fired upon from another post and suffered casualties. Though unhurt, Simpson and his sergeant dragged their wounded comrades into the post, killed the surrendered Germans and settled down to defend their new position.[38] Although clearly under fire from the enemy, was Simpson's predicament such that the captured Germans posed a threat to his command's safety? If they were not, it was clearly an abrogation of his responsibility to the conventions of International law. If they posed a valid threat, then a case for military necessity might be advanced but men having surrendered must surely have justifiably believed themselves beyond such consideration. Bean, at any rate, does not enlighten us as to why they were killed.

Private L.F. Hann, who was captured by the Germans at Villers-Bretonneux, declared unreservedly that the 33rd Battalion had orders to capture and consolidate the enemy's front line 'but to take no prisoners'.[39] That he was able to make that statement at all shows that he, at least, was not subject to the same unlawful treatment.

That Bean was able to faithfully record such incidents without any comment about the obvious implications they had for the civilised conduct of warfare may have reflected a journalistic detachment from his subject. It was clearly not an oversight but a practised style. The possibility exists, too, that, having already stated his position in the earlier volumes, he did not feel compelled to comment on similar incidents in the later volumes. Throughout the official history, Bean – even if his personal point of view was otherwise – was content to absolve Australian soldiers from any blame in regard to breaches of the Hague Rules and British military manuals in regard to inhumane treatment towards the enemy. Bean believed the men could not be held accountable because they had not initiated the war and they were, through the white heat of battle, as much victims as those to whom they occasionally showed no quarter.

Four

'Go on, you haven't killed one yet...'

Comprehensive as Bean's volumes of the official history were, they were not the only body of work in which the subject of killing and mistreatment of prisoners was broached. The postwar period saw the publication by battalion associations of numerous battalion histories designed to record, for posterity's sake, the contribution of those units that had served in the First World War. Many of these would mirror Bean's attitude about the Australian soldier. Some were candid in their accounts, while others were circumspect in what they said. Others omitted any reference to the issue at all.

Written most often by ex-battalion officers, with a view to preserving and perpetuating the reputation of the Australian soldier, it was never likely that these accounts would be particularly incisive or critical of what they revealed. Also, given that many of the manuscripts were submitted to Bean for comment, it is possible that some of the official historian's attitudes were incorporated on revision. Nevertheless, the battalion histories canvass a range of issues not engaged by Bean in the official histories.

Some battalion histories clearly communicated the impression of an uncompromising attitude when they came to close-quarter grips with the enemy. The 30th Battalion history described an action in which one of its patrols surprised a German minenwerfer crew. Two Germans were captured and the remaining six members of the post were 'suitably disposed'.[1] A 17th Battalion raid was regarded as entirely successful after killing an estimated thirty Germans and capturing four, one of whom was killed as he was escorted across no-man's land because he became 'recalcitrant'.[2]

Another incident from the 17th Battalion's history, involving

Private E.C. Ralphs, is worth citing for the ethical dilemma it posed for soldiers captured in battle. Ralphs was captured and disarmed with another man, Private A.R. Saundercock, when their post was overrun. Two Germans escorted Saundercock to the rear and a third motioned to Ralphs to follow. As soon as the German turned his back to continue his advance, Ralphs seized a rifle and shot his captor and made good his escape. Here was a trust by one soldier to another, perhaps naïvely offered, being betrayed. Prisoners under the Hague Rules were entitled to make good their escape. The danger of sending prisoners back unescorted is clearly demonstrated by Ralphs' action. He had not become so inert as to accept his surrender as a fait accompli. Fortuitously, Saundercock, too, made his escape when his escorts were shot down. He returned to the Australian lines eventually only to find his mates had given him up for lost and already divided the contents of his haversack amongst themselves![3]

The trust or assumption made by Ralphs' captor was one displayed and betrayed on both sides. Lieutenant 'Joe' Blacket, 27th Battalion, who on observing the arrogance of a particular German officer thought it best to intervene and protect the man lest his attitude provoke the Australians into acting intolerantly. He ordered the officer to be taken to the rear as a prisoner, at which point the German produced a pistol and shot Blacket at point blank range, killing him instantly.[4]

Though Bean would likely have bracketed the German officer and Ralphs acts as 'brave', even if at the same time an act of perfidy, the men in the line saw them as nothing more than the basest form of treachery. Presumably, the German officer was killed in turn. The net result of such behaviour, as the authors of the 27th Battalion history suggested, was only to help 'considerably to create a feeling of disgust and contempt towards the enemy'.[5] Such incidents naturally undermined the process of rational thought required to apply generosity towards the enemy in accordance with the rules of war. An officer of the 27th Battalion who shot seven prisoners with his revolver, after a corporal had refused to do so, was certainly proof of that ugly process.[6]

Nevertheless, the desire to slaughter the enemy did not always override the desire to preserve their lives. Australian soldiers in the

38th Battalion charged with the task of clearing the enemy dugouts uttered German phrases to the effect of 'It is alright' to encourage the enemy to surrender. It was as often as not ignored by men frozen by indecision and Mills bombs were then tossed into the dugouts to root out the reluctant defenders.[7]

One aspect in both the official histories and the battalion histories that sits incongruously with the descriptions of the actions described is the high body count reported in some raids in relation to the amount of prisoners taken. Consider the following passage from the 38th Battalion history describing a raid carried out in conjunction with the 37th Battalion at Warneton in early 1918:

> When one comes to consider the fact that at least 100 of the enemy garrison had been killed (including the Company Commander), 33 taken prisoner, and much booty...he cannot but come to the conclusion that the operation ranks as a brilliant success... The results obtained by our men in the face of strong opposition by a resolute enemy must compare favorably with any similar operation throughout the Division, even in the whole Australian Corps. Our casualties (38th Battalion) totalled six...[8]

Does this small total, when compared to the German losses, equate with losses one would expect in the face of strong opposition by an enemy that fought resolutely? Even allowing for the fact that the barrage had caused some damage, and conceding some element of exaggeration, the German losses appear excessive. Are such descriptions indicative of language disguising a killing spree? Did the Australians simply allow no quarter?

Similar questions might be asked of other accounts. The 41st Battalion undertook a raid in which five Germans were killed at a cost of no casualties to the Australians, even though 'the hostile post offered strong resistance'.[9] In detailing the first raid of the 4th Division, Newton Wanliss frankly admitted that the German casualties given were an overestimate but added that '[t]heir casualties probably contained many killed, for little quarter was given, and it was impossible under the circumstances to bring back prisoners'.[10]

The practice of 'no quarter' was undoubtedly tacitly approved at higher levels of command. The language of the 2nd Brigade commander about a combined 7th and 8th Battalion raid conveniently provided the smokescreen for a slaughter. He stated,

> I am informed by those concerned that the enemy all fought well and doggedly, and live prisoners were therefore impossible to procure. Every German fought till he was killed with the exception of one wounded...[11]

The attached 7th Battalion report does not quite support such an unequivocal conclusion as to the impossibility of taking live prisoners. Three of the Germans were shot without any apparent attempt to take them prisoner and another bayoneted when the signal to withdraw was given.[12]

The desire or need to kill the enemy was often diluted in the larger set-piece battles such as that fought on 8 August 1918. The whirlwind bombardment that preceded the surprise attack and the appearance of tanks in the advancing allied line saw large numbers of Germans surrender without offering any resistance. The ease with which these men were claimed made it difficult for even the most hardened souls to act despicably. Surrender even in these circumstances had its dangers. The need to make one's intentions clear over the clattering tanks and general noise of battle could, one imagines, have led to animated signing that could easily be misinterpreted.

Subsequent lines might also misinterpret the sight of large bodies of the enemy passing rearward as advancing opposition forces. In recounting the September 1918 battles, the authors of the 1st Battalion history stated that, of the 100 prisoners taken, not all reached the rear.[13] The nature of their fate is not disclosed. Whether victims of Australian brutality or of the counter-barrage or some other mishap is immaterial to the general understanding of the ongoing dangers the battlefield held for surrendered men making their way rearward.

The large numbers of prisoners being taken in the final push of 1918 often proved embarrassing to the Australians, many of whose units were under strength. A single soldier more often than not would be put in charge of escorting up to twenty prisoners to the rear. Prisoners, once captured, generally had conceded to the point where thoughts of escape were little considered. Depression, bewilderment and shock often accompanied surrender and contributed to the passivity of the prisoners, who were as often as not just happy to be getting away from the fighting. However, sometimes when large batches were captured they realised the vulnerability of their captors after their initial fright had subsided. When about fifty to sixty Germans willingly surrendered to a three-man patrol from the 37th Battalion, a German officer attempted to rally his men, forcing the Australians to fire into the crowd, scattering them in all directions, before making good their own escape.[14]

At Pozières, 11th Battalion men prepared to accept the surrender of some Germans who raised their hands in submission only to see a German officer or NCO dash along the trench beating down his men's upraised hands. Hostilities were resumed.[15] Lack of unanimity and confusion among defenders was not conducive to encouraging attackers to risk coming forward and accepting an uncertain surrender.

A grim reminder of that risk was the death of Lieutenant Harold Thompson, 14th Battalion, during the August offensive 1918. Having signalled to a party of two dozen Germans to surrender, some of whom raised their hands, Thompson went forward, only to be shot in the head and mortally wounded. His platoon went forward and concentrated their fire on the 'miscreants', all of whom were killed, wounded or scattered.[16]

The history of the 3rd Battalion is the most damning of the battalion histories in regard to questions of no quarter. Its account of the attack on Bayonet Trench on 5 November 1916 raises a number of issues. The bomb and bayonet work that was proudly described also shows that giving quarter was simply not countenanced. Privates Weger and Maker were the first two bayonet men and were instructed to 'start the dirty work'. The 'dirty work' was the killing of the unlucky survivors in the dugouts after a bomb had been thrown in.

The pressure on inexperienced men to engage in this standard practice was also immense. One man with less experience than his comrades reported to his sergeant that he had found a German in a shelter. He was told to 'fix' the German but replied that he could not kill a man that way. The sergeant's reply was devoid of morality and compassion: 'Go on, you haven't killed one yet; I'll give you one more chance and then I'll fix him myself.'[17]

To his credit, the man did not compromise his stand and it was left to the sergeant to kill the hapless German. When the soldier had said he could not kill a man that way, he meant he could not kill a man in cold blood. The victim was clearly beyond the point of being a threat. In all likelihood, he would have attempted to convey some sign that he wished to surrender and to plead for mercy. There was no justifiable military reason to kill him. However, the men had been addressed prior to the fight by Lieutenant Loveday and told that the upcoming battle was 'an excellent opportunity to avenge the death of their colonel'. Lieutenant-Colonel Howell-Price had been mortally wounded a few days beforehand.[18] Killing as retribution was something that was specifically outlawed in the Hague Rules.

During this assault by the 3rd Battalion, one German, at least, was captured. He was described as 'smaller than the others' and able to speak some English. His diminutive stature (and youth possibly), along with the fact that he could speak English, appear to have contributed to his survival. Yet he was an exception. Worse still was the fact that the Australians also murdered wounded Germans in their care. Sergeant Yorke, who was asked to take a message back to headquarters, agreed, adding laconically, 'All right, I'll go back through the trench and fix up those — Huns, their moaning has been getting on my nerves.' When the order finally came to retire, the small German prisoner was carried back but other prisoners were euphemistically noted to have gone 'for a stroll'.[19] The incident is corroborated in the diary of Sergeant A.E. Matthews:

> Orders came through from Brigade for us to evacuate our position and to leave no live Germans behind. Guessing that there would be dirty work for somebody killing the wounded prisoners, I and a Lance Corporal volunteered to escort the two unwounded prisoners back to Battn Hqrs and we had just got away when we heard the awful screams of the men who were being slaughtered through military necessity.[20]

For their heroic conduct in this attack, Weger and Meaker received the DCM, Loveday the Military Cross, and Yorke, too, was recommended for an award by the brigade commander.[21] If, as

Matthews states, the orders to kill the enemy wounded emanated from brigade headquarters, then the Australian brigade commander at the time, Brigadier-General Heane, is deserving of condemnation, the more so because as a senior officer there could have been no question as to his misunderstanding the rules of war. From how far up the chain of command such orders were being issued remains problematic.

A captured soldier's fate was very much determined by the conscience of his captor. Men of upstanding nature obviously posed no threat to a prisoner. Those who had descended into the moral abyss that war created were less predictable. Sometimes the two came into conflict. Colleagues lying on the start tape prior to an attack observed the fate of a 3rd Battalion soldier at Ypres. The Australian had inadvertently advanced alone into the bosom of the enemy. Although one German gesticulated to the effect that he wanted to cut the Australian's throat, another emphatically resisted and escorted the Australian to a nearby pillbox. The 3rd Battalion man was able to return the favour to his captor when the Australians subsequently captured the pillbox.[22] Opportunity to indulge so specifically in such an act of mutual obligation was rare.

It could be argued that Australian soldiers adopting ruthless attitudes towards their enemy were responding directly to stimuli from the High Command. Despite the codification of the rules of war in British army manuals, 1917 marked a significant shift towards re-emphasising the spirit of the bayonet in British psychology in an attempt to inculcate a greater blood lust in the Empire's soldiers. The redirection was sarcastically noted in the history of the 37th Battalion:

> It appeared that, in the absence of any better strategic plan, our superiors had decided that the best way to win the war was by killing Germans.[23]

The circumstances of a man's capture undoubtedly contributed to the likelihood of his survival. The further removed from warlike activity or the more absurd a situation appeared to the men, the less likely was it that darker sentiments would override decency. For example, when four soldiers of the 2nd Battalion dozed off at their post and were overrun by the enemy, one of the men woke to find a German with a bayonet pointed at his throat (and possibly a smile upon his lips).[24] Similarly, Sergeant Morrison, 5th Battalion, was able to capture two men with some bemusement; one was asleep and the other was found packing his kit. Though these men and other prisoners displayed an unwillingness to move along the parapet to the Australian trenches, their recalcitrance did not inspire Morrison to kill them. Instead, he opted for a more creative and humane solution and moved them along by throwing clods of dirt at them.[25]

The 5th Battalion history offers further examples of men responding to their prisoners' reluctance, not with summary execution but with methods that were, even if a little heavy-handed, designed to encourage rather than kill or maim. One German sergeant who refused to leave his dugout proved more amenable after an Australian private 'put the boot into him', he and his comrades' journey to the rear being further hastened by their escort firing several shots into the ground behind them.[26]

If frayed or jaded nerves were responsible for men acting irrationally or inconsistently when confronting the enemy, then, as always, officers on the spot had the greatest influence. Some, as we have seen, set a ruthless example. Others, like CSM Crooks during a 45th Battalion excursion into the enemy trenches that secured a large number of prisoners, opted for humour to keep the men together.[27] Light-hearted banter, even in the most hazardous of environments, could calm men and appeal to the gentler and more reasonable side of their personality.

A further element contributing to the safety of captured men was the importance of being able to establish communication clearly with one's captors. This was made all the more difficult by the barrier of language. In this, as has already been mentioned, Germans were better served than the Australians. The 5th Battalion historian pointed out that 'a good proportion' of the German soldiers captured at Glencorse Wood 'and nearly all their officers, spoke English tolerably well'.[28]

The inability to communicate clearly, as well as the sense of shock at being challenged unexpectedly by the enemy, proved fatal, though perhaps unnecessarily so, for one group of four Germans who came into contact with the 14th Battalion. Having clearly lost their way, they walked leisurely past Australian wiring parties into the Australian lines. On reaching the Australian parapet, the leading German was challenged. He 'apparently being too bewildered to surrender, was promptly shot dead'. One is tempted to ask why, if he was so obviously confused, it was necessary to kill him. A bomb followed and the other three surrendered.[29]

Morality could and often did prevail over baser sentiments on the battlefield. A 41st Battalion soldier who had acquired a prisoner at Messines, despite having lost his rifle and bayonet, requested the loan of a weapon to 'despatch the intruder'. The author of the 41st Battalion history considered this a reasonable request by a 'right-thinking man'! However, the man's mates did not 'see eye to eye with him in the matter' and refused. Disgusted by this, the Australian soldier then forced the German to partake in a souveniring expedition using him as a guinea pig to taste edibles found in surrounding pillboxes until an officer rescued the dragooned food taster.[30]

Though the incident is advanced as a humorous anecdote, it is instructive in displaying the existence of and conflict between differing attitudes held within the ranks. The fact that officers of the 41st Battalion's intelligence staff compiled the book and considered the man's initial intent as 'right-thinking' is further evidence of the ambivalence that existed in regard to appropriate treatment of prisoners.

The battalion histories provide alternative incidents to those recounted by Bean and, to a degree, confront the issue of killing prisoners more openly. Like Bean, however, they refrain from judging Australian soldiers' behaviour. And as the examples drawn from the 3rd and 41st Battalion histories show, such action was, in fact, condoned. In that respect, they represent a marked departure from Bean's attitude.

Five

'It's no good, sonny, there are too many of them, we will have to surrender'

To comprehend the complexity of Australian soldiers' experiences in close-quarter combat, one must necessarily move beyond Bean's official histories and the quasi-official nature of the battalion histories. The diaries and letters of soldiers provide some insights, yet by far the greatest source for individual soldier responses is those contained in the repatriated prisoner statements. Some of these statements were used by Bean in compiling the official history and are contained in AWM 30 of the Australian War Memorial's collection. These were statements taken from prisoners on their return from imprisonment. The statements sought to establish, for the amy's record, information about where and how the prisoner was captured, the circumstances that brought about his capture, which officer ordered the surrender and, finally, to establish the nature of the Germans' treatment of their prisoners. These questions evoked a range of responses, some exceptionally detailed and others less so.

The official nature of the statement undoubtedly tempered some responses. There were other reasons that could also be countenanced for the men's reluctance to offer much detail. The ignominy of being captured was perhaps too great for some and they preferred to give only the barest outline of events. Bland statements may have also masked unheroic actions. Understandably, few soldiers were likely to admit to personal weakness or lack of fortitude. This was a courtesy they may have extended to others.

It was rare (but not unknown, as will be shown) for soldiers to criticise other men in the repatriated prisoner statements. A sense of solidarity is pervasive. However, they were less sanguine in their references to officers whom they felt had not stood by them. Sergeant J.F. Ryan, captured at Dernancourt, condemned his company officer, Captain Hird, who he claimed 'did not show himself once and remained in his concrete dugout during the whole of the attack'. He also accused the No. 1 platoon leader, Lieutenant Rolls, of remaining 'out of harms way'.[1] Although Ryan's defence of his post appears in the official history, his criticisms of his officers do not.[2]

Private W.P. Seward revealed a sense of abandonment coupled with marked disdain for an unnamed Australian officer in his statement:

> An officer passed us and asked 'Have you plenty of ammunition left?' I answered 'Yes.' He said 'Use the bloody stuff and give it to 'em.' In the meantime he was clearing out of harm's way as quickly as he could.[3]

One soldier who was damning in his appraisal of his colleagues was Private L.J. Farrington, 54th Battalion, who was captured at Hollebeke in late November 1917. Farrington was blinded as a result of the fight and perhaps had reason to be more bitter than most. His repatriated statement is unusual in that he categorically names those who contributed to his misfortune:

> After a brief pause the Huns threatened another assault... There were fifteen of them at the most... I glanced in the direction of Cpl. McGrath and Pte. Love, and saw them crouching about 10 yards distant under the cover of the galvanised sheet of iron and the protection of the side of the depression. Pte. West was at the opposite end of our 'possy' and ready for the attack. I called to the Corporal. 'Look out they're coming again.' He did not answer. Again I said 'Come on, get at them with the Mills.' We had a plentiful supply of bombs and I reckon there would have been a very different tale to tell had the corporal and Pte Love elected to fight. Certainly at the first surprises they had fired a few shots, but now they had the wind properly up. McGrath answered 'It's no good sonny, there are too many of them, we will have to surrender'. 'Not for me' I said. Love 'chipped' in with 'What's the use? Think of your life.' In the meantime the gun team on our right had decamped without ever attempting to put up a fight. I was properly disgusted and determined to see it out.[4]

Farrington's statement is a far cry from the usual accounts about Australian aggression and mateship. There is a touch of self-aggrandisement in his account and it must also be noted that an individual's perceptions formed in such an intense situation may rely on assumption and be ill-informed. The gunners may have been ordered back. Irrespective of these things, Farrington's account points to a quite logical variability in men's morale. Disagreements as to what course of action to take, the loss of aggression and the consequences emanating from such things were vividly outlined. It would be ridiculous to think Australian soldiers were immune to the eroding effects of deteriorating morale. Once blighted by its corrosive nature, defensive positions were unlikely to be held.

It was obvious that, as situations deteriorated or as the men's nerve began to fail, some discussion of surrendering took place. When the enemy was spotted 100 yards in the rear of the 46th Battalion, Sergeant C.D. Burton stated that some of the chaps began to talk of surrender. When the enemy did break into the position, Burton noted that the sight of his wound was enough to persuade a German to desist from the act of throwing a bomb at him.[5]

The decision to surrender was, not surprisingly, a bone of contention for soldiers in the front line who had arrived at different conclusions as to what best to do. At Bullecourt, CQMS A.L. Guppy, on seeing six men endeavouring to hoist a white towel on a bayonet, ordered them to stop. On being asked what they should do, he replied that he didn't really know. He offered two alternatives, either attempt to run back to the Australian lines, through the intense barrage and the crossfire that swept it, or remain and be captured. Neither seemed much of an improvement on the original intention of the six men.[6] In the absence of any meaningful plan of escape, Guppy's reaction appears to have been merely an indignant expression in response to the unpalatable thought and act of surrender through the showing of a white flag.

The most common reason given by Australian soldiers for becoming a prisoner was that they had run out of ammunition. Such declarations permeate the statements by repatriated prisoners. It was a theme that Bean reiterated throughout the official history, along with the suggestion that most were wounded. It was certainly not a reason advanced to describe German surrenders to Australians. Australian narratives from all sources are unanimous in depicting German prisoners as tossing the towel in to save themselves while uttering 'Kamerad, Kamerad' to signal their capitulation. Indeed, the 'Kamerading' Hun is a caricature that was presented for Australian merriment (along with the docile Tommy) in both wartime and postwar soldier accounts, trench newspapers and unit histories. Most soldiers in all armies were captured through a combination of their military position becoming untenable (or through the perception that it had) and a loss of fighting spirit. Unpalatable as it may be to Australian sensibilities, Australian soldiers sometimes surrendered because they had become demoralised and lost the will to fight.[7]

Once soldiers knew their position was compromised or untenable, the sight of an enemy with a revolver in one hand and a bomb in the other at a dugout doorway was usually enough to prompt surrender.[8] When one side was attacking or counterattacking, its soldiers were often preoccupied with the need to push on to objectives that saw captured prisoners ignored or sent back without escorts. The latter was, as we have seen, one of the reasons proffered for killing prisoners under the contentious principle of military necessity. Yet throughout the war thousands upon thousands of men were sent back, at least initially, in this manner. One suspects that men just captured were in such a recognisable dazed state as to be considered a non-threatening presence. While some soldiers, like the previously mentioned Private Ralphs, refused to accept the act of surrender as a binding contract, it would seem most did.

It is obvious in some of the postwar statements of repatriated prisoners that the ignominy of surrender still burned. Some statements were almost certainly made to cast the best possible light upon those caught by the enemy. The 53rd Battalion was one of the first Australian units to have lost heavily in this manner at Fromelles. Statements by some of its members demonstrate the variance in attitudes towards surrender. Some acquiesced and accepted their fate. For others, the act still rankled. Lance-Sergeant A.L. Harrison stated, 'Just after break of day a white flag was hoisted to my right... When the order to surrender was given our case was hopeless.'⁹ From where, from whom and why the order to surrender emanated was of central importance to the questions asked of repatriated prisoners. Private P.J. Gill stated,

> I observed the officer commanding our company (Captain Ransom) with a white flag raised and the other men of the company throwing down their arms and surrendering. I was with another man and we decided that as the survivors of the company were surrendering we had better do likewise.¹⁰

Another 53rd Battalion man recorded his and his comrades' surrender with unbowed and obstinate pride (and a hint of denial). Prefacing his comments with the facts that the mud had rendered their rifles useless, the ammunition was expended and no detonators were available for the bombs, Corporal J.E. Morris declared, 'These men never surrendered, but were helpless and taken prisoners against their will. I did not see one man with his hands up.'¹¹

The circumstances as to how soldiers became prisoners, while often similar, varied in detail. Ruses sometimes played a part. Command of the English language allowed Germans to more readily entice inattentive or unsuspecting Australians towards them. At Warlancourt, Sergeant W. Chappell, 28th Battalion, was captured when he heeded English voices urging him to come on towards them. He did so and to his surprise he found himself in a German post covered by a hostile bayonet.¹² Fear of firing upon one's own led to the capture of a party of 50th Battalion soldiers at Noreuil. They claimed the Germans advanced on them while parading a group of prisoners before them, leaving the group with no alternative but surrender or shoot down their own.¹³

The act of surrender was also a potentially hazardous exercise. For example, men trapped in dugouts wishing to surrender were caught in a form of purgatory. They were hardly encouraged to surrender by the merciless treatment sometimes dished out to those brave enough to venture up first. Sappers caught in a dugout at Laventie (near Fleurbaix) in late May 1916 witnessed the first of their number shot and the second bayoneted before an English-speaking under-officer arrived at the sap head and called for the rest to come out.¹⁴ Nor can the knowledge of the nature in which trench raids were conducted have been a comforting thought for those captured and held in dugouts.[15] Counterattacking comrades were unlikely to be expecting their own troops to be occupying the dugouts that they were bombing.

For many men, lying doggo was the most practical action to adopt once wounded or cut off, or if they had lost their aggression. The unwounded or those only slightly wounded might attempt to make their way back to their own lines under cover of darkness. If close to their own lines, they might be fortunate to have a patrol or stretcher-bearers come by. Those trapped close to the enemy line relied on enemy kindness to give them succour. It does seem that, as the curtain of night fell on the daily drama of the front line, men assumed a less aggressive frame of mind. This was not surprising, given the likelihood that hostilities for the most part ceased at night. Nevertheless, the parlous nature of the front during heavy fighting meant that men were not guaranteed discovery, and many must have perished unattended.

Private W.J. Baldock, 21st Battalion, was lucky in that respect. Having been rendered insensible by a shot through his neck and spine, he was placed in an old dugout with a number of dead men. There he remained for five days until found by a German officer and his men.[16] After spending days isolated in no-man's land, it was of little consequence whether a rescuer was friend or foe. Private R.E. Membrey, who had become disoriented in the fighting at Mouquet Farm and had spent two days without food and water, was one who was 'not sorry when a German patrol spotted us and took us back'.[17]

The moment of capture was also the moment in which a complete and utter shift in power took place. It was the moment when the equality of fighting men transferred to an unequal one where the captor was elevated to dominant status and the captive to a level of enforced submissiveness. It was the moment when the decision of life and death moved beyond the control of the captured man to his reliance on the goodwill and mercy of his host. It was a new relationship that required some psychological adjustment.

The twilight zone soldiers entered on being made prisoner is described by Captain J.H. Honeysett:

It would be safe to aver, however, that the question of falling into the hands of the enemy was very seldom considered by the average British soldier. After months of more or less drab routine of trench warfare in France, and constant association with khaki clad comrades, suddenly to find oneself amidst an excited crowd of grey clad, strange speaking foreigners was an experience which leaves one at a loss to describe. I can well remember, however, the one peculiar impression which I gained during those startling moments of my capture. It seemed that I had already shared the fate of my many good pals lying in the trench and that I had entered a new world, and, strangely enough, this weird mental obsession remained with me until after my first sleep as a prisoner of war.[18]

Another to express the anguish and psychological adjustment was Lieutenant V. Garnet Veness, also captured at Bullecourt: 'I have experienced[d] the sorest and bitterest feelings of my life within the last few days. I remember in various letters at having spoken slightingly of men who were captured and now I form one of the band.'[19]

For Corporal Lancelot Rawes Dawes, captured at Bullecourt, surrender was the 'most humiliating experience of a lifetime'. For Dawes, fear quickly departed after the initial humiliation and shock of capture subsided, even though his journey back saw him strafed by the belated British barrage, fired on by British planes, taunted and molested by souvenir hunters. His thoughts were all concentrated on the uncertain future before him and the 'trek into the unknown'.[20]

For both sides, the change in circumstance was all the more difficult following unexpected contact. Lieutenant N.D.L. Cumming, 22nd Battalion, considered his captors to be 'just as annoyed and dumbfounded' as he was until they realised they had the upper hand.[21]

It was at the moment of capture and during the exodus from the front that prisoners were most vulnerable and some men carried the uncertainty of incidents they had witnessed into their post war lives. Corporal H. Ford, who had observed an attack on the tram line at Noreuil, wrote after the war, 'I saw some chaps jump into the trench and have often wondered if they were murdered, or whether they were taken prisoner.'[22] This long-standing doubt also implied that the likelihood of captured men being murdered was a scenario soldiers knew they or others might have to confront. It implies it was a practice in common use.

The examples we have seen of Australian mistreatment towards German prisoners make the task of accepting Australian claims about their own mistreatment all the more believable. At Lagnicourt, a large number of 11th Battalion men were captured when almost a full company was cut off. The men were removed to the German first line and searched. Private K.S. Ross became a victim of treacherous behaviour as he moved to the rear. While hurrying to catch up to his officer between the second and third German line, a German soldier cut him off and shot him through the left breast.[23]

It was a barbarous act and certainly not an isolated one. A number of statements by men captured at Fromelles mention incidents in which surrendered or surrendering Australians were shot down. Private A.D. Stone claimed two of his comrades were 'shot down in cold blood' after they had surrendered.[24] Corporal McKee of the 54th Battalion suggested brutality on a wide scale. McKee was captured at Fromelles and believed that 'many Australian dead...had been killed whilst prisoners by the Germans, for, nearly all of them were shot through the head'.[25]

Another 54th Battalion man related an incident that goes some way to sustaining the possibility of McKee's assertion: 'After being taken prisoner we were fired on and suffered several casualties.'[26] Private H.R. Putt, 51st Battalion, claimed a similar fate for some of his comrades:

> About 17 of us were taken prisoners and after being disarmed we were taken towards the rear. While going into the German communication trench I saw eight of the party shot by the German sentry.[27]

Private S.F. Cubis described the fate of a 26th Battalion gunner during the thrust and counter-thrust of battle at Lagnicourt:

> L/Cpl Brown, of 'A' Company, was shot from behind by a German as he was walking away from the gun. I could not say whether he was killed or not but he was badly hit in the body. This happened after we were captured.[28]

Another 26th Battalion man confirmed that Brown was killed while under escort by a machine-gun bullet, but offers no comment as to who fired the fatal shot.

Comment of ruthless acts was not limited to just those of the enemy. One of the more cold-blooded acts, if it can be said there are degrees to such things, was that of a sergeant major of the 48th Battalion. His callous act is described in the testimony of Private P.J. Liddy, who was captured during the attack at Bullecourt:

> Our Sergeant Major, a new man that I did not know, shot a German soldier to obtain a souvenir. The soldier put up his hands and pleaded for mercy, but he was shot dead and the Sergeant Major took his field glasses.[29]

Having passed through the first arduous experience of surrender, subsequent interrogation could prove harrowing. Private H. West, when asked about the position of the Australian artillery, found himself being battered about the head by stick-bombs with the accompanying message, lest he hadn't worked it out, that he would be forced to give the information.[30] Men of the 17th Battalion found themselves 'badly knocked' about at Lagnicourt, as it was apparently explained to them, for not surrendering sooner. The diary entry of Private F. Klingner revealed a similar experience:

> I was taken separate from the others to a cellar in Dernancourt. On being questioned there I was threatened to be shot for refusing to tell them anything. By this time I was feeling the worst after being blown up once by a shell and then lying in water for 10 hours. I received my first introduction by a knock on the back with a rifle butt which just about ruined me altogether.[31]

A 51st Battalion man 'rounded up' at Fromelles was Sergeant L. Ramshaw. Contrary to the testimony of many other Australians, he saw 'nothing amiss' in the treatment of the Australian wounded and his interrogation by a German medical officer proved somewhat amusing:

> Are you an Englander?
> No, I'm an Australian.
> You're a liar! – Australians are black!

Whether the officer was being mischievously ironic or displaying rank (or perhaps understandable) ignorance, he at least used no force or threats of violence in pursuit of information.[32]

Ramshaw may have been lucky, as the admission that one was an Australian seems to have been provocative at times. Private F. Curtis, who surrendered during the fighting a Dernancourt in April 1918, was shot through the stomach by a German officer after answering a question as to his national identity. According to Private J.A. O'Rourke, who witnessed this 'cold-blooded act of murderous brutality', Curtis had been unarmed and had given 'no provocation whatever'.[33] Private Victor Savage, also among the Australian prisoners captured at Dernancourt, was punched in the mouth and his false teeth broken when he admitted to being Australian.[34]

Some of this treatment meted out to captured Australians may have been due to an apparent reputation for ruthlessness that preceded them. This was something that had been played up by both German and British propaganda and which was confirmed through some of the indiscreet acts connected with the Australian method of waging war. Sergeant J.S. Tomlinson, who was captured at Bullecourt, was told – as his captors did 'a bit of a war dance' around him – that he 'ought to have been shot as our boys don't take prisoners'.[35]

That the Australians had come so far to fight what was to the Germans a European affair no doubt confounded some Germans. It was both a source of bemusement and anger judging by some responses. Private Nelligan, 32nd Battalion, recorded that a German officer, who was unable to understand why Australians had got involved in the war, called him and his friends 'sheep stealers'.[36]

Rough treatment after capture was a common experience, though not necessarily the pervasive one. Often it represented a perverse form of gamesmanship and was clearly designed to exacerbate the prisoner's anxiety. Violent intimidation was also undertaken, on occasion, with the intention of encouraging prisoners to give information. This was done despite the fact that prisoners were not required to divulge any such information and was probably the most widely disregarded rule of war. The more common method of interrogation was to imply that other prisoners had provided information in an attempt to draw a prisoner into making a statement.

Of course, at both the moments of capture and during interrogation, a prisoner could exert some influence on his situation through compliance and/or passiveness. At the moment of capture, some men were overcome with the desire to bolt. Whether this was one's instinct of 'flight' kicking in or a reckless show of bravado is difficult to tell. Whatever it was, it was an act fraught with danger. Private A.E. Park described two officers being promptly shot down as they attempted to make a break at Mouquet Farm. Park was one of thirteen who had taken refuge in a shell hole and one of five '[e]ventually...taken from that shell hole as prisoners'.[37] Again we are presented with an ambiguous statement. Were some of the Australians cruelly done in or had battle casualties taken a toll?

Some soldiers clearly did not enhance their prospects for survival by being overtly combative. A captured Australian officer who began firing wildly with his revolver during the act of taking off his equipment was spared only because the outraged German officer displayed 'chivalrous restraint' wrenching the pistol from the Australian with a warning that he could have shot him for such an injudicious act.[38] The German's chivalry is a tonic to the conduct of civilised warfare. If he was able to display such restraint under extreme provocation, then the defence of accepting the inevitability of acts that contravened the laws of war is even less convincing.

Chivalry and common sense sometimes blended to make the act of surrender a less demeaning process. As a party of Germans advanced on Private L.J. Briand and others at Bullecourt, one of them shaped to throw a grenade. On seeing Briand with two grenades and ready for action, the German tossed his aside, where it exploded harmlessly near the parapet. Briand did likewise. The Germans then moved forward to capture the Australians with recourse to unnecessary violence averted.[39]

Lieutenant O. Flight of No. 2 Squadron, AFC, was lucky not to be killed after being shot down. He was allowed to return to his plane on the pretence of collecting his watch. Instead he fired his Verey pistol into his machine and set it on fire. The Germans fired upon him and only the intervention of one of their officers saved the Australian.[40]

Failure to put one's hands up was also a risky business, as Private James Egan attested: '3 men were shot by the Germans because they had not got their hands up.'[41] It would also seem it was no guarantee for captured men. At Fromelles, adding to the list of alleged German cruelty there, Private Thomas Bolton declared he had seen men shot after they had placed their hands up.⁴²

Perceived breaches of the rules of war could raise the wrath of one's captors. A case in point was those caught in possession of questionable ammunition. The soldiers of both armies were particularly sensitive to the use of expanding bullets which had been expressly outlawed in the Declaration of St Petersburg 1868 and broadened to incorporate the banning of dumdums in the Hague Rules 1899.⁴³

That Australians used these cruel instruments is certain, given the reactions by some captured officers. Captain Honeysett considered himself to be lucky to be alive after 'a few rounds of that particularly venomous looking blunt-nosed missile' were found in his ammunition pouch. Honeysett thought his captor's anger was fully justified and was only rescued by the timely arrival of a German officer.⁴⁴

British ammunition was a contentious issue on other occasions for the Germans. Captain D. Wells' captors threatened to shoot him after examining a few rounds of ammunition found in his pocket, which they declared to be of the dumdum variety. He argued his case stating that the ammunition was approved and authorised by the British government. This calmed his captors to a degree, though it was evident that they were not wholly convinced, replying that it was the nearest approach one could wish for, and that 'the British are not playing the game by using it'.⁴⁵ Corporal L.D. Brooks captured near Ypres was another treated roughly over the allegation that his service revolver ammunition was dumdum.⁴⁶ The ammunition in question was most likely the flat-nosed Cartridge, SA, Ball, Revolver, .455 inch, Mk IV. Introduced in 1909 and approved in 1912, even the War Office admitted to it being 'ugly' and appearing 'inhuman'. It was withdrawn in late 1914 and replaced with what was hoped to be a less provocative Mk II version.⁴⁷

The journey to the rear and away from the front line was also a precarious one for captured men, although the likelihood of them being killed certainly diminished the further they got from the fighting. The Germans appeared to be less thorough or avaricious in their pursuit of souveniring compared to the Australians' legendary penchant for the game. Although a prisoner's personal property was not meant to be taken from him, it was clear that a process of exchange was sometimes invoked to supplement worn items. Private G. Abbott, 18th Battalion, who was captured at Hangard Wood, commented, 'Our boots were taken from us and old and worn German boots given us in exchange.'[48]

Private C.H.E. Duncan also had his boots taken, along with his puttees, overcoat and identity discs, before being put to work cutting grass for the German cavalry horses stationed behind the lines.[49] Private William Quinn, 53rd Battalion, was similarly stripped after capture at Fromelles, though he lost his shirt too and was left half-naked.[50] Quinn's treatment was unusual but not surprising, given numerous statements about the savagery of the German Uhlans who escorted Australian and British prisoners to Lille after the battle. They pushed and kicked wounded men, rode down sympathetic French citizens who called encouragement to the despondent captured soldiers and generally made themselves a nuisance.[51]

Prisoners were confronted by variety of behaviour from their captors during and after the moment of surrender. The fluctuations in this, and trying to discern what was the norm in a new and uncertain situation, must have caused a degree of paranoia towards those of the enemy they met in the journey rearward. Two Germans beckoned Private B.J. Healy, 51st Battalion, into a trench and made him their prisoner. In a scene more suited to the Mad Hatter's tea party, one offered him a coffee while the other made threatening gestures with his fist.[52]

For the wounded, capture presented an even more uncertain time than those not incapacitated. Capture was a welcome relief and avenue for survival for some such as Private L. Gosewinckel, who was captured at Bapaume, and was 'almost frozen' and 'too far gone to help' himself'.[53] For others, though, a wound proved a death warrant. A badly wounded 23rd Battalion man was shot by a German officer despite the appeals by other captured Australians that they were willing to carry the unfortunate soldier.[54] Was the officer committing an act of mercy or was he merely despatching a man whom he considered an encumbrance? Either way, his actions are not supported in the rules of war.

The fragile state of the wounded and the parlous zone in which it placed them is further illustrated by the account of a 38th Battalion soldier captured at Houplines near Armentières:

> I waited behind to bring in a wounded companion who became delirious and got on his hands and knees and shouted. The enemy opened fire and killed the wounded man... I tried to retire but found that the Germans were behind me. They covered me and I had to give up.[55]

Corporal Stuart, 25th Battalion, wounded in both legs was brought in by two Germans, one an officer, who then knocked him senseless with the end of a rifle butt.[56] Private C.H. Kennedy, by contrast, was well treated by his capturing officer, although his treatment was less satisfactory behind the lines. At Cambrai, he claimed that a German major deliberately aggravated his wounds with a three-pronged surgical instrument, grandstanding before a score of grinning assistants, saying, 'I love to see you suffer, you're an Australian not an Englishman.'[57]

Men of the 15th Battalion who were captured after clearing the dead from the recaptured trenches were witness to a grim undertaking:

> We had to remove our wounded who had been left in the barbed wire, those who had leg wounds and could not walk were shot with a revolver through the head.[58]

Private A.T. Nelligan, who was captured at Fromelles, gave the following emphatic account that suggests treacherous behaviour by Germans bearing Red Cross armbands. He described the fate of a fellow soldier who, after attending to a wounded mate, approached the German lines to surrender and seek assistance for his friend:

> A German whom he approached – I took him to be a German Red Cross man and an officer – shot him through the head with a revolver. This murderous brute had some stretcher-bearers with him... Anyhow that is what he did. I saw him.[59]

The use of Red Cross armbands as a ruse appears to have been a feature of German tactics in 1916. If discovered, the Germans ran a risk of inflaming their captors to react in retribution to such subterfuge, as Archie Barwick of the 1st Battalion recorded:

> This afternoon we got 15 German Red Cross prisoners, they were marched down & searched & 13 of the dogs were found to be carrying daggers & revolvers they [were] promptly put against the wall & finished.[60]

The misuse of Red Cross armbands, as well as the efficient and merciless proficiency of German raiders, feature in an account by Corporal D.W. Austin of the embarrassing raid in which the new Stokes mortar was captured from the 20th Battalion near Bois Grenier on 5 May 1916:

> Every man of this raiding party was wearing a Red Cross band on the arm and were all armed with revolvers and a sort of life preserver which was a square piece of metal about 2lbs weight, attached to a handle of spring steel about 18 inches long. This was a formidable looking weapon, and capable of smashing in a man's head. They also carried hand grenades and each man had a electric torch attached to his breast. When Simpson was pulled out of the dugout, I heard a shriek. I never saw him again. I think he was hit in the head with one of those weapons and killed before I got out of the dug-out. I did not hear any shot fired. He had been badly wounded and could not walk.[61]

At Bullecourt, incapacitated men of the 48th Battalion were certainly recognised as non-threatening. A German sergeant who was first to discover one Australian party asked in French, 'Blesse?' On being assured that all were wounded, he passed on with a smile, returning later with some comrades to attend their prisoners.[62]

Kind treatment administered by the Germans was a surprise to some. Private George Hilton, captured at Mouquet Farm, thought '[t]he treatment the enemy gave me was far better than I had expected'.[63] One can only guess at what expectations of treatment existed in Hilton's mind. Doubtless they were shaped by a combination of propaganda, trench rumour and, perhaps, mistreatment of German prisoners that he had witnessed. In fact, for many of the men captured at this stage of the war, German medical treatment towards the wounded was courteous and efficient with little distinction made between friend and foe. Australian prisoners were inoculated against lockjaw at the dressing stations behind the lines.[64]

The sight of wrecked bodies and the plight of unattended wounded lying amongst the wreckage of battle was still in evidence sixty-odd years after Henri Dunant had been inspired by such human misery. The relief of wounded soldiers in the First World War was especially difficult given the static nature of the war. Irrespective of whether a soldier was shot down in no-man's land or on entering the enemy's trenches, he remained vulnerable in contested ground, because the armies did not move on. His evacuation was a difficult task and the speed of the initial clearance of the wounded was determined by the availability of the usually overworked stretcher-bearers and/or enemy prisoners to assist. Soldiers could also be left for dead with a complete absence of malice. Private L.J. Kinna recounted a story told to him by Private W.P. Seward, 48th Battalion, who was captured at Bullecourt and was hurried off by his captors before he had an opportunity to dig out and rescue a soldier buried by an explosion.[65]

Australian accounts of the treatment of their wounded varies from the sympathetic and humane to the callous and barbaric. Incidents of murder have already been discussed. To them may be added incidents of neglect and rough handling. Some charges were no doubt misinformed and the disregard of the enemy wounded was sometimes due to the need to fulfil other priorities. Treatment and clearance of one's own wounded and the need to consolidate newly won or breached positions were obvious examples. Nevertheless, some rough treatment was clearly avoidable.

At Bullecourt, Captain D.P. Wells, 13th Battalion, considered the German medical orderlies to have brutally handled the Australian wounded, with a total disregard for the nature of their wounds. He also claimed his captors made a wounded comrade drink paraffin, resulting in the soldier's death soon after and that they attempted, with no success, to force the vile liquid down his throat. He further stated that the wounded were robbed and left unattended with no effort to remove them to safety and believed 'hundreds must have died through exposure and wilful neglect'.[66] Lieutenant William Stones was wounded at Bullecourt and was detained for two days without any attention. Only after he managed to get a letter of complaint delivered to the company officer was treatment forthcoming.[67]

Yet it cannot be said that the Australians themselves had a spotless record in this regard. An Australian medical officer recorded his anger at finding an unattended group of badly wounded prisoners sporting such wounds as penetrating [sic] (protruding?) abdomens, fractured femurs and skulls. On sending word back to the company officer about the plight of these men, that officer informed him that he was not going to make his exhausted stretcher bearers do any more work. Finally, men from the 1st Field Ambulance were approached and kindly obliged to relieve the Germans' distress. The angered medical officer concluded,

> ...the incident raises an interesting question as to the lengths we should go in the collection and treatment of enemy wounded. Personally I think that here, where there was no special risk attached to the attempt (though certainly a considerable amount of extra fatigue) it was right to treat these men as the human beings they were, not as so many wild beasts.[68]

The journey rearward for captured men presented other obvious dangers. When undertaken through one's own barrage it could, and often did, result in more casualties.[69] It could also mean rough handling by the enemy troops one passed. Rifle butts, fists and feet were used as a means of venting frustration and anger at the prisoners. Private John Bolton claimed that one wounded man died as a result of the violent treatment meted out at Fleubaix.[70] Private A.A. Stephens, wounded and captured at Bois Grenier, was bayoneted in the leg as he was being taken down a communication trench. His journey was the cause for further bad treatment at the end of a rifle butt following the outbreak of artillery fire on the German position.[71]

Corporal L.R. Dawes, who was wounded, observed some of his fellows being struck with rifle butts and prodded with bayonets and fully expected to be shot as a German sighted his rifle on him. He managed to draw an officer's attention to the man, who was immediately ordered away. Soon after, he received what he described as 'one of the worst beltings that it was possible to give a man', which left him unconscious for four hours.[72]

The straitened circumstances the men found themselves in and the insecurity they felt was always alleviated somewhat by contact with others who had fallen victim to the same fate. Corporal Harry Andrew Still, who had run the gauntlet of souvenir hunters and the kicks, punches and spittle of his bayonet-probing Bavarian hosts at Fromelles, was relieved and able through conversation to regain some sanity on meeting his wounded company officer.[73]

The personal statements and narratives of Australian soldiers clearly demonstrate a variety of experiences that confirm, not only that they indulged in unlawful killings and mistreatment, but also that they were victims of such treachery and abuse.

Six

Gerfangener

Having survived the initial contact with the enemy and then been ushered out of the front line, Australian prisoners, or 'gerfangeners' as the Germans termed them, entered a new experience. The uncertainty that existed in men's minds about their fate as a prisoner of war has already been discussed. As the experience of interned Australian soldiers sits outside the real focus of this brief study, the intent of this chapter is to draw some attention to a subject that is sorely in need of greater research as well as providing some understanding of a prisoner's lot beyond the battlefield.

The Australian prisoner of war experience remains a relatively unexplored area in Australia's First World War history. By contrast, the prisoner of war experience of the Second World War, by virtue of the large numbers of Australians captured by the Japanese, coupled with the horrors endured, has seen that experience embedded into the national psyche as arguably the dominant national memory of that conflict.

The most recent research exploring the experience of Australian prisoners of the First World War is an unpublished paper, 'In the Hands of the Hun: Australian Prisoners of the Germans in the Great War', by Rosalind Crone, a summer scholar at the Australian War Memorial in 2002. As with this book, the repatriated prisoner statements contained in AWM 30 provide a central source of evidence for that work.

Just as treatment and reactions of the enemy varied at the initial point of contact, so too was there a variation of experience in captivity among Australian prisoners. Brutality and unnecessary hardship was a fact of life for many First World War prisoners. Crone's work clearly proves her assertion that at times,

71

[I]t would not be unreasonable to state that these conditions could be comparable to those suffered by Australians in Turkey, and later by Australians under the Japanese in World War Two.[1]

One of the first undertakings by the Germans when dealing with batches of prisoners was to separate the officers from the men once they reached the marshalling areas in the rear. The laws of war at the time made clear distinction between the treatment of officers from the ordinary rank and file. The rationale for this lay mostly in the time-honoured traditions respecting rank and privileges that existed within the officer corps of European armies. Officers were treated better than their men. Such separation also had an immediate and, perhaps, detrimental effect in that it deprived the men of leadership within their group at a moment when it was probably most desired to assuage anxiety about their predicament.

Officers were generally transferred to officers' lagers, while other ranks found themselves dispatched throughout Germany and its territories in working commandos. These sometimes saw them working close to the front line. Officers, on the other hand, enjoyed the protection from such menial deployment under the rules of war. The men were put to work in coalmines, salt mines, and stone quarries as well as being sent into the forests as lumber workers.

As noted previously, a consistent grievance in Australian statements and narratives of men captured at Fromelles in 1916 and Bullecourt in 1917, was of the brutish behaviour of the German cavalry escorts, the Uhlans, towards both prisoners and civilians. For the men captured during the Fromelles and Bullecourt fighting, this rough treatment was compounded by a suffocating incarceration at Fort MacDonald in Lille, where they were kept in overcrowded, damp and unsanitary conditions for several days. Fort MacDonald was dubbed the 'Black Hole' or 'Hell Hole'.[2] However, as Crone points out, the bulk of prisoners at Fort MacDonald were considered 'Prisoners of Respite' by the Germans, in response to alleged mistreatment of their own prisoners at the hands of the British.[3]

Private L.W. Keirnan of the 54th Battalion, who was captured at Fromelles, believed the Germans were conscious of wanting to create a scene of utter humiliation as a means of undermining the confidence of the local populations and the prisoners themselves. As such, he and others were the subject of a theatrical display following their surrender whereby their clothing was 'cut about' by the Uhlans to make them 'appear ragged and badly clothed'.[4]

A further explanation for the crude behaviour of the Uhlans may be that they were not active front line troops and so had little empathy for their captured opponents. Although front line troops were, as we have seen, quite adept at meting out retribution on occasion, it appears that they did not engage in such behaviour as uniformly as the Uhlans. As Corporal Harry Still commented in regard to his internment,

> The best and most reliable guard was the returned man, one who had seen for himself that which had been our portion. He was the most sympathetic and there was a mutual understanding, almost friendship, between us.[5]

Harry Still's narrative of his capture at Fromelles and subsequent experience is a useful one for providing a general picture of the lot of a prisoner of war. Following his removal from the front line, he was transferred to Lille. During the march, he fainted and was transferred to a tramcar, under guard, as he was too weak to continue on foot. At Lille, he was subjected to the cramped conditions and poor food (a small piece of black bread and a pint of watery maize) and fancied himself in a similar predicament to the prison's inmates during the French Revolution. After interrogation and a few days incarceration, he was entrained, forty prisoners to a truck, on a two-day journey through Belgium to a prison camp near the small town of Dulmen in Westfalen. The prisoners were permitted to spend their money en route, purchasing small cakes and other treats at the various railway stops.

The camp at Dulmen was ringed by a double row of barbed wire. The men were divided into companies and assigned to basic huts that housed fifty men in double bunk beds, although a small cubicle and separate beds were provided for the NCOs. Still spent a month at Dulmen. Rations were poor and the men lost weight rapidly and were affected by dysentery. Smokers were forced to go cold turkey and the day began at 6 a.m. with roll call and ended with the same at 7 p.m. with little to do in between time.

Still was next moved by train to a camp at Minden. This was a camp exclusively for NCOs. Although Still claimed the conditions were better, the diet remained unsatisfactory and his weight continued to fall, plummeting in his estimation at three quarters of a pound per day from 13 stone 4 pounds down to 8 stone 9 pounds. His first Red Cross parcel arrived ninety-three days after his capture and thereafter on a fortnightly basis, from which time things began to gradually improve. There were fifteen nationalities in the camp and the inmates engaged in teaching their respective languages to others. An occasional camp newspaper was provided, as was musical entertainment. Winter, despite its severity, offered alternative entertainment through ice skating and snowball fights. Yet boredom still prevailed and the men had to combat the danger of becoming 'stir crazy' or contracting 'gerfangenitis', as they termed it.

After twelve months at Minden, Still was transferred by train through Germany to a camp at Soltan near the Denmark border. Before entry into the camp, the men suffered the peculiar process of having every hair on their body shaved. It was a portent of what was to be a stay punctuated with harsh treatment under the auspices of the camp commandant, Uber Leutnant Mueller. According to Still, Mueller was gaoled for six months after the war for his mistreatment of prisoners. At Soltan, the men were put to work beyond the confines of the prison, clearing bracken from the moors, digging peat and planting potatoes (a crop which they managed to effectively sabotage). Fortunately for Still, he was released under the agreement between England and Germany that allowed prisoners of war of more than eighteen months to be exchanged.[6]

Starvation, overwork and violence from the guards form the kernel of grievances by Australian prisoners. While these at times reflected the inexplicable penchant for aggression and degradation that man is capable of, Crone argues throughout her paper that poor treatment also reflected the decline in German fortunes as the war progressed. Food and medical supplies became less accessible as the blockade and war effort took its toll. As well, Germany's diminishing manpower reserves saw a greater reliance placed on prisoner labour.

The Red Cross played a vital role in supplementing the bland diets of prisoners that often compromised of little more than poor quality bread, sauerkraut or weak soup. By the latter part of the war, the Germans, too, were suffering acute shortages. Despite this, it seems that the foodstuffs provided in Red Cross parcels were passed on without interference, even if delays sometimes occurred in their distribution. This was a source of wonder to many Australian prisoners. Jim Wheeler, captured at Bullecourt, recalled,

> One thing I must admire those Germans for, starving themselves, and they let those tons of parcels come through untouched without thieving anything.[7]

The other vital area in which the Red Cross was involved was in organising the exchange of badly wounded prisoners or of men deemed psychologically unable to survive captivity. An agreement to affect this exchange had been forged early in the war. It usually meant the transfer of the wounded men to the neutral countries of either Holland or Switzerland for the duration of the war.

The protection of the Red Cross, however, was limited and it was inevitable that some men suffering through psychological breakdown or mental illness would not receive appropriate attention. Private Frank Comery, a 16th Battalion man captured at Bullecourt, recalled the suicide of a 48th Battalion soldier:

> He had been working behind the German lines and there had sustained severe shell shock. He was put in the 'REVIELLE' (observation hut) and while there was supposed to be looked after by Belgian orderlies. Somehow he got hold of a razor and in the latrine, cut his throat. He died while being carried to the lazarette. We brought wreaths and got the German parson to read the prayers at the grave side. Some of us Australians were at the funeral. [He] had previously asked the German orderlies for poison but they only laughed at him.[8]

As can be seen through these few examples, the lot of Australian prisoners was not without considerable hardship. Few prisoner of war accounts were produced by returned 'gerfangeners'. Some such as Reg Sanders broadcast their experiences on public radio but by and large it remained and remains a largely neglected aspect of AIF history.

Conclusion

Arriving at a conclusion as to why men allowed themselves to kill surrendered or wounded enemy soldiers is a problematic exercise. Certainly, the desensitising intent of propaganda played with effect on some men's minds. The military's cultivation of blood lust through bayonet training also reinforced the generally negative views being aired about the enemy. We can say that some, though not necessarily all, men were influenced by this training. Some clearly recognised the malevolent intent of the training and propaganda.

A positive to be drawn from the evidence examined, at least from a humanitarian point of view, is that even in the face of orders from above or from immediate superiors, and despite their military training, many men refused to engage in the practice of killing illegitimately. Occasionally this did not save the unfortunate soul whose life was being threatened. Another soldier or the officer issuing the order was likely to step up and finish the 'job'. Sympathetic as many were to their enemy's plight, he was still the enemy and those despatching prisoners illegally were still on your side. Friend or foe were the keystones to the business of war and confronting one's own about the killing of the enemy was a dilemma which most chose to avoid. It was probably a hollow comfort for men to be able to say they had not indulged in murder, knowing that their personal moral stand did not influence the actions of their mates. Some, of course, were successful in protecting threatened prisoners.

That some men were able to resist the temptation (if that is what it was) to kill the enemy in cold blood was commendable. That choice was a moral one and the men who made it ought to be applauded for acting humanely. Ultimately, the responsibility of committing an act of treachery came down to the individual. In praising those men's actions, should we denounce as treacherous the acts of those who did kill in cold blood? Can we make excuses, as C.E.W. Bean did, that it was the architects of war who ought to be condemned, not the men who fought them?

Without doubt, war created an atmosphere and an anarchic world in which sordid human behaviour found expression. Flawed individuals, for whom killing provided some perverse pleasure, possibly existed and thrived in the environment of the front line. Much as one would hope that they represented an insignificant percentage in any of the armies, the extent and widespread incidents of killing do not allow us to dismiss the recorded actions of some soldiers as abstract aberrations. We must share Bean's suspicion that there were rather more incidents than we wish to think about.

According to Swank and Marchand's study of Second World War soldiers, two per cent of enlisted men were predisposed to be 'aggressive psychopaths' who suffered neither the resistance to killing or psychiatric disorders associated with killing that occurred in other soldiers. In citing this statistic, David Grossman cautioned his readers not to prejudge these men with modern-day connotations. He argued that they do not represent a set of psychopaths or sociopaths but, rather, a percentage of the male population that 'if pushed or given a legitimate reason, will kill without regret or remorse'.[1] They represent a distinct minority but one which, Grossman argues, had 'a capacity for the levelheaded participation in combat that we as a society glorify and that Hollywood would have us believe that all soldiers possess'.[2] Such men are, arguably, indispensable to any army or nation in time of war.

These men may well have been representative of the stronger types that Bean claimed resided in greater numbers in the Australian Imperial Force than other armies, though on that point neither he nor we could ever know.[3] Irrespective of their numbers, those who killed indiscriminately or illegally were more likely to reside in that minority group. It may be purely coincidental that Australian soldiers feature in the worst examples of treacherous behaviour cited by John Keegan in his study of men in battle and in triumphal participation in Grossman's account of killing at close quarters with the bayonet. Grossman cites an Australian soldier's letter to his father: 'Its good sport father when the bayonet goes in there eyes bulge out like prawns [Sic]'.[4]

The question such anecdotal evidence prompts is whether Australian soldiers were more inclined than others to engage in such killing. We know from many studies of the First World War that the soldiers from all armies, at times, engaged in the practice of killing surrendered men or refused to take prisoners. Australians were both perpetrators and victims in the process. Whether more so than others is impossible to determine. Bill Gammage believed Australians were 'among those most willing to kill' and that they had been sufficiently conditioned by negative propaganda to hate with a loathing almost unparalleled in the British Army.[5] Whether true or not, there is certainly enough evidence to suggest that national and international level propaganda promoted a distinct image of the Australian soldiers as an uncompromising warrior which was believed by German soldiers and which has certainly been readily incorporated into Australia's national military mythology. The downside of such an aggressive image may have been the promotion of a level of savage reciprocity, as Bean had feared, with each side believing the worst of the other.

A central plank in Grossman's study of killing is the degree to which society and the army (as an extension of that society) work to desensitise people to acts of violence. The more one is desensitised, the more one is likely to be receptive to the act of killing.[6] This process is most evident in the Australian experience through the aggressive propaganda that unrelentingly depicted the enemy as a blood thirsting beast, killing and raping innocents. How successful it was in turning soldiers' minds is unmeasurable, though something of its spitefulness is perhaps reflected in the ungenerous terms that some Australian soldiers used to describe the enemy. The terms 'squareheads' and 'Huns' were popular. The Australian soldier who wrote approvingly of the actions of his officer in killing two wounded Germans because they were supposed 'baby killers' suggests a marked success for the propagandists.[7] At the army level, the blood lust encouraged in training, particularly from 1917, quite deliberately set out to condition soldiers to the task of killing the enemy intimately. The British and Australian armies willingness to engage in this is hardly surprising. Soldiers who cannot kill are a liability to any armed force.

A refreshing aspect to have emerged from studies by S.L.A

Marshall, Swank and Marchand and contemporary historians such as John Keegan, Richard Holmes and David Grossman is that soldiers have, over time, displayed a marked resistance to killing – particularly at close quarters.

While killing at close quarters in a legitimate combat is desirable and acceptable, the killing of prisoners and the practice of 'no quarter' cannot and should never be condoned. Yet it was practised and it was advocated by British and Australian officers. The encouragement of 'no quarter' was not limited to local or small unit commanders. The bayonet training and blood lust promoted through the language of the army manuals and propaganda all implicate higher authorities in the process. The ambivalent advice pertaining to the 'do's and don'ts' of treatment towards enemy prisoners expressed in information distributed to the men can hardly be interpreted as anything other than providing a blind eye approach to transgressions of international law.

The encouragement for men to show no quarter in battle represents an obvious disjuncture in the policy of national government and its military extension. The humanistic and diplomatic efforts in peacetime by governments to secure and codify basic human rights for soldiers through the Hague Conventions was in many instances undone by the, at times, unfettered self-governance of the army in wartime. It is here that the lesson resides for governments to be accountable for and vigilant of their military representatives.

The 'heat of battle' argument that men, once programmed to kill and in the grip of a cocktail of emotions that combat engendered, could not be expected to turn off or be able to think rationally, has some legitimacy. Yet always stacked against it is the fact that some men, and the large numbers of prisoners taken overall would suggest many, did display the necessary emotional intelligence to act kindly and in a humane and lawful way.

There is no doubt, however, that the pressure to show no mercy was most intense at the small unit level. Again, the problematic nature of the evidence makes it difficult to make any substantive claims. One must refrain from claiming that 'no quarter' was a tacit doctrine throughout the AIF. However, it is clear that attempts were made to instil an ethos at battalion level. Mottos of 'Wipe Out The Bloody

Germans' had no other purpose than to cultivate a hatred towards the enemy. That some leaders at the company and platoon level practised such an ethos is also supported in the evidence. A philosophy of '[t]he only good German is a dead one' expressed by a company officer of 1st Battalion, provides a further suggestion of an uncompromising attitude, even if one inspired by personal revenge.[8]

Combat officers represent one group who possessed the capability, the authority and, one would expect, the intellectual capacity to directly influence behaviour. Milgram's famous laboratory experiment in which subjects were manipulated under direct orders to inflict seemingly lethal charges of electrical shocks upon their pleading and screaming victims is an obvious model for comparison. A staggering sixty-five per cent continued to obey orders to inflict the simulated shocks despite their victims' apparent unconsciousness or death. Important factors to consider in the subjects' willingness to continue were the proximity, respect for, intensity of demands by and legitimacy of the authority figures.[9] If Milgram's results can be translated directly to the battlefield, then soldiers in the presence of an officer demanding no quarter would most likely have submitted to his demands.

Many soldiers, quite understandably, would have acceded to their officers' demands to kill prisoners or refuse surrender. The hierarchy of command and the expectation of lower ranks to defer to authority as demanded by the British *Manual of Military Law* make it a likely response. The 3rd Battalion incident at Flers provided a stark example of officers and NCOs imbued with the ethos of killing methodically and dutifully despatching wounded prisoners. Yet the incident also revealed men resisting the unlawful act. The soldier who refused to kill a man in cold blood provides an example of open defiance. The soldiers who opted to escort a prisoner back in preference to murder provide a more common, indirect and easier method of avoidance. Of course, neither action saved the Germans in question; they prove, however, that soldiers had a capacity to oppose or resist authority in such instances.

Unfortunately, too many officers, though certainly not a majority, were not of a mind to curb such behaviour. They clearly encouraged it and, it would seem, sometimes rewarded perpetrators with military decorations. Schooled in the laws of war and conversant with British army regulations, there exists little room to make excuses for recalcitrant officers. Their job was to command and control and their failure to rein in men engaged in indiscriminate killing was culpable. It is difficult to see how Australia's senior officers could have been blind to the practice. Official reports of raids with kill tallies disproportionate to those captured cannot have escaped the attention of senior commanders.

The defence most often used to justify the murder of enemy prisoners and wounded was the claim of 'military necessity'. In the case of the wounded, this simply has no substance. Men incapacitated and disarmed were of no threat to any force vacating or occupying a position. To kill them was simply murder and indefensible as a legitimate act.

On a more positive note, the evidence we have examined also provides accounts of Australian officers who, contrary to the blood lust sometimes manifest in their peers and men, did intervene and save prisoners from an uncertain fate. Also, Australian repatriated prisoner statements are peppered with accounts of diggers being saved from rough handling during their capture by the intervention of English-speaking German officers.

It would be naive to suppose that soldiers were always placed in a position where they could spare the enemy. A case for killing fractious and panicked prisoners could, depending on the circumstances, be argued as justifiable military necessity, but only if the safety of one's own command was placed at risk by their behaviour. Men under enemy attack or trying to make good their own escape could easily feel compromised if valuable time had to be expended in convincing prisoners to move on. However, most prisoners were as keen to vacate the area as their captors were and often the rudimentary tactic of a well placed boot or cuffing was enough to persuade any recalcitrants.

In the larger set-piece battles, escorting prisoners to the rear was usually planned for. It was the introduction of the trench raid and its permanency in the battle tactics on the Western Front that compromised the rules of war as they stood in 1914–18. Killing the enemy became a strategic objective rather than a consequence of battle. This form of warfare was a response to the stagnation of meaningful movement and an expression of the generals' frustration at the constrictions that modern warfare had produced. The limited time allocated to these lightning raids placed surrendering soldiers in an invidious position. Protective barrages were laid down, and the need to escape before they were lifted was paramount to the raiders' own survival. Large batches of prisoners could certainly inhibit movement. It was in the raids that verbal and sometimes written orders capped the number of prisoners required. This inevitably produced a situation where no quarter – even though illegal – was regularly invoked.

It was also apparent that uncertainty about the intentions of the enemy towards prisoners was something men carried into battle with them. Niall Ferguson has suggested that victory in the First World War finally turned on the Allies' ability to take large numbers of prisoners rather than kill large numbers of the enemy. He is wary of accepting the 'war weary' explanation for the dramatic turnaround in German fortunes that began with the Allied offensive in August 1918. The reason why so many Germans began to surrender, he admits, is 'elusive' but the suggestion is that attitudes to and by the enemy to surrender had something to do with it. That is, the Germans became less afraid to surrender because the British became more tolerant to captured or surrendering men. Ferguson inclines to the view that, had either side encouraged the other to surrender rather than generating an atmosphere of distrust and paranoia about the enemy, perhaps the war would have finished earlier.[10]

The Australian disposition towards the enemy in 1918 supports Ferguson's point of view. Although the unlawful killing of prisoners in all likelihood continued until the end of the war, the number of incidents probably reduced. From June until their withdrawal from the line in October 1918, the taking of prisoners became a new badge of honour for Australian battalions as they vied with one another to match or better the exploits of neighbouring units. This attitude was most noticeable during the period known as 'peaceful penetration', in which Australian patrolling and raiding secured large numbers of prisoners and continued into the breakthrough battles where a newfound willingness to surrender was often noted by the Australians. The fact that many of the German soldiers were by that time unseasoned youths also possibly explains their willingness to surrender, as well as an unwillingness on the part of the Australians to kill them.

It is unlikely that we will ever see a war fought as the First World War was. The wizardry of modern technology and the destructive capacity of modern missiles and bombs despatched from a distance, particularly with a dominant ally such as America boasting a near unassailable military might, make it unlikely that large numbers of Australian citizen soldiers will be called to war. Occupation and specialist forces will, however, still come into contact with the enemy. The government that despatches these men overseas has a duty to ensure that they are properly tutored in international law and that they are not programmed by deceitful propaganda and training methods as was practised during the First World War.

During the First World War, both the British and Australian governments failed their soldiers by not having their hands sufficiently on the levers controlling the military. British and Australian generals and junior officers failed their men by deliberately ignoring international law sanctioned by both the government and, supposedly, the military they served. In this respect, Charles Bean's charge that the authorities who make war ought to be held accountable not the soldiers themselves might be upheld.

We can make many excuses for soldiers acting in an unlawful manner in the hellish conditions of the front, suffering exhaustion, primed by the hate-mongering of their officers and fearful of their own survival. We should not lose sight of those things. There has been a tendency, however, to use these as a blanket apology to ignore and defer scrutiny of such unlawful acts. While some soldiers can be excused of blame in certain incidents due to the confused nature of circumstances at the time, others cannot. The fact that some soldiers could refrain from unlawful killing and did see it for what it was – cold-blooded murder – makes acceptance of such reprehensible acts more difficult.

That Australian soldiers engaged in the practice of killing enemy prisoners and giving no quarter is undeniable. So too is the fact that Australians were victims of this practice. Killing in this way was widespread in the First World War. In saying it was widespread, one cannot say that it dominated behaviour on the Western Front. Large numbers of prisoners were taken during all major battles and the practice was most likely at its worst during trench raids that involved relatively small numbers from both sides, though when repeated over and over a rather grim tally is accumulated.

A criticism of Joanna Bourke's work is that, in collating a body of so many despicable acts, it fosters a sense that soldiers killed rather gratuitously and easily in such circumstances. Perhaps this work, too, might be criticised along those lines. However, nothing could be further from the intention of this book. As Grossman, Holmes and Keegan have demonstrated in recent times, men suffered great remorse over killing. This is backed up by the large numbers of soldiers known to have suffered psychological trauma during and after the war. Not all was shell-shock-related.

People who hold the heroic motif of the digger of the Anzac legend dear to heir hearts may well resist the idea that Australians could act in so unsporting a manner. Acknowledging Australian participation in this facet of the First World War is important. It reveals the cruel and sordid underbelly of the conflict from which we, as a nation, draw so much inspiration. We can be justifiably proud of many of the achievements of the Australian army in that conflict. We should also be appalled by the fact that Australian officers and British military authorities encouraged and sanctioned unlawful acts of killing surrendered enemy soldiers and encouraged no quarter in battle.

As a nation, we should be conscious of what we ask and expect of our soldiers in combat. While the pressure of combat in the front line is immense and, for most, unimaginable, we have seen that soldiers were capable of resisting demands or pressure to kill unlawfully. Others could not or chose not to. Australia's First World War soldiers were asked to obey orders that ran contrary to both international law and to their own army's regulations. In that sense, Bean was right: blame can be justifiably laid at the feet of war's architects. The tendency to excuse Australian soldiers for acting in such a manner, based on Bean's premise and by citing what are regarded as legitimate excuses of military necessity or the 'heat of battle', has obscured the fact that many acts were avoidable and, worse, were quite deliberately planned and enacted.

Soldiers do have to accept some responsibility for their own actions in combat. It is not a responsibility they should bear alone. Supposedly enlightened and civilised nations ought to endeavour to protect their armed servicemen from the compromising effects of debasing propaganda. Soldiers need to be educated about the pitfalls associated with illegitimate behaviour so that they are given the best possible chance to make the right decision in combat. War may be hell but fighting men need not don the cloak of the Devil.

Notes

Introduction

1. C.E.W. Bean, *Official History of Australia in the War of 1914–18: The AIF in France 1916*, v. III, Angus & Robertson, Sydney, 1936 [1929], p. 514.
2. *Ibid.*
3. *Ibid.*, pp. 514–5.
4. *Ibid.*, p. 514
5. *Ibid.*
6. John Keegan, *The Face of Battle*, Jonathan Cape, London, 1976, pp. 48–9, 51.
7. Bean, *Official History of Australia in the War of 1914–18: The AIF in France 1917*, v. IV, Angus & Robertson, Sydney, 1933, p. 772.
8. *Ibid.*, See, n. 115.
9. W.D. Joynt, *Breaking the Road for the Rest*, Hyland House, Melbourne, 1979, p. 129.
10. Keegan, p. 51.
11. Bean, v. IV, p. 772, n. 115.
12. Peter Charlton, *Pozières*, p. 136.
13. *Ibid.*
14. AWM 27, 424/12
15. John Monash, *The Australian Victories in France in 1918*, Lothian Book Publishing Co. Pty Ltd, Melbourne, revised edition 1923 [1920], p. 229.
16. Ross McMullin, *Pompey Elliott*, Scribe, Melbourne, 2002, p. 647.
17. Letter undated, Gellibrand to Bean, Bean papers 3DRL 6673, 419/8/1.
18. Letter dated 18 March 1918, Bean to Gellibrand, *ibid.*
19. They were found not guilty of killing a missionary (Heese) of German extraction although it is likely that their execution was a means to appeasing the German government over Heese's death.

One

1. Donald A. Wells, *The Laws of Land Warfare: A Guide to U.S. Army Manuals*, Greenwood Press, Westport, Connecticut, 1992, p. 79.
2. *Ibid.*, p. 80.
3. *Ibid.*
4. *Ibid.*
5. Carl von Clausewitz, *On War*, Penguin Classics, 1968 [1832], p. 102.
6. Gretchen Kewley, *Humanitarian Law in Armed Conflicts*, VCTA Publishing, Melbourne, 1984, pp. 3–6.
7. Wells, *op. cit.*, p. xiii.
8. *Ibid.*, p. 22.
9. *Ibid.*, pp. 80–1.
10. *Ibid.*, p. xi.
11. *Ibid.*, p. 6. The US neither signed nor ratified this declaration.
12. Kewley, *op. cit.*, p. 7.
13. The bullet took its name from the arsenal at Dum Dum near Calcutta, India where they were first produced.
14. *International Law Concerning the Conduct of Hostilities: Collection of Hague Conventions and Some Other Treaties*, International Committee

of the Red Cross, Geneva, 1989, pp. 24–5.
15. Robin S. Corfield, *Don't forget me, cobber: The Battle of Fromelles 19/20 July 1916: An Enquiry,* Corfield and Company, Rosanna, Victoria, 2000, p. 455. Relevant portions of the manual have been reproduced on pp. 453–63.
16. *Ibid.*
17. Joanna Bourke, *An Intimate History of Killing: Face-to-Face Killing in Twentieth Century Warfare,* Granta Books, London, 1999, p. 177.
18. Capt. J. H. Honeysett, narrative, AWM 3DRL 4043, 1 of 3, p. 18.
19. For example, the circular 'Prisoners of War', Xth Corps No. I.G. 33/36, dated 20 March 1915 in AWM 27/424/5.
20. AWM 27/424/7
21. Capt. E. Gorman, *With the Twenty-Second: A History of the 22nd Battalion, AIF,* H H. Champion, Australasian Authors' Agency, Melbourne, 1919, pp. 9–10.

Two

1. C.E.W. Bean, *Official History of Australia in the War of 1914–18: The Story of Anzac: The First Phase,* v. I, Angus & Robertson, Sydney, 1941 Twelfth edition [1921], p. 258.
2. *Bulletin,* 23 September 1915.
3. Bean, v. I, p. 259
4. *Ibid.,* pp. 420–1.
5. Recorded by Sgt Fred Carthew in a letter dated 25 May 1915 cited in Noel Carthew, *Voices from the Trenches: Letters to Home,* New Holland Publishers, Sydney, 2002, p. 95.
6. Greg Kerr, *Lost Anzacs: The Story of Two Brothers,* Oxford University Press, Melbourne, 1997, pp. 1–3.
7. Bean, v. I, p. 420.
8. *Ibid..* see fn 18.
9. Bean, v. I, p. 267.
10. Kevin Fewster, *Gallipoli Correspondent: the frontline diary of C.E.W. Bean,* Allen & Unwin, Sydney, 1983, p. 83.
11. *Ibid.,* pp. 82–3.
12. *Ibid.,* p. 83. For an example of NZ'ers fighting with their gloves off see Bean's reference to the bayoneting of 20 Turks on Destroyer Hill during the night advance on Sari Bair, Bean, v. II, p. 570.
13. C.E.W. Bean, *Official History of Australia in the War of 1914–18: The Story of Anzac: From 4 May 1915 to the Evacuation,* v. II, Angus & Robertson, Sydney, 1936 fourth edition [1924], p. 221.
14. Typescript copy of the diary, 28 June 1915, Pte. D. B. Creedon, 9th Battalion, AIF, AWM 1DRL 223, file 12/1/86.
15. Fewster, p. 149. Entry for 8 August 1915.
16. *Ibid.*
17. Phillip Schuler, *Australia in Arms: A Narrative of the Australasian Imperial Force and their achievement at Anzac,* London, T. Fisher Unwin, 1916.

Three

1. Peter Dennis et al, *The Oxford Companion to Australian Military History,* Oxford University Press, Melbourne, 1995, p. 473.
2. Commonwealth of Australia, *German Atrocities: Germany and Inhumanity: Humanity and Christianity,* The Director General of Recruiting, Victoria Barracks, Melbourne, 1917.
3. Operation Order No. 2, by Lt-

Colonel A.B. Stevens, DSO, CO Raid, 12 October 1916.
4. Papers of Sgt A. E. Matthews, 3rd Battalion, Copy of diary, p. 25.
5. For a discussion of soldiers' reluctance toward this mode of killing see Grossman, *On Killing: The Psychological Cost of learning to Kill in War and Society*, Little Brown Books, New York, 1996 [1995], pp. 120–30.
6. Bean, *Official History of Australia in the War of 1914–18: The AIF in France 1916*, v. III, Angus & Robertson, Sydney, 1936 [1929], p.248
7. *Ibid.*, see n. 10.
8. *Ibid.*
9. *Ibid.*, p. 248.
10. *Ibid.*, p. 250.
11. *Ibid.*, p. 249.
12. *Ibid.*, pp. 249–50, n. 10.
13. *Ibid.*, pp. 260–83.
14. *Ibid.*, pp. 362–3, n. 40.
15. *Ibid.*, p. 442.
16. *Ibid.*, p. 418–9.
17. *Ibid.*, p. 422. n. 84.
18. *Ibid.*, p.436.
19. *Ibid.*, p. 437, n. 121.
20. *Ibid.*, p. 440.
21. *Ibid.*, .p. 499.
22. *Ibid.*, p. 541.
23. *Ibid.*
24. *Ibid.*
25. *Ibid.*, p. 717. These were the men Albert Jacka's party would later rescue in a bold charge that led to his near fatal wounding and which was roundly considered worthy of a second VC.
26. Bean, *Official History of Australia in the War of 1914–18: The AIF in France 1917*, v. IV, Angus & Robertson, Sydney, 1933, p. 110.
27. *Ibid*, p. 219.
28. *Ibid.*, p. 339, fn 180.
29. *Ibid.*, p. 504.
30. *Ibid.*, p. 629.
31. *Ibid.*, p. 766.
32. Pte C H. Kennedy, statement, 2 December 1918, AWM 30, B5.15B
33. Bean, *Official History of Australia in the War of 1914–18: The AIF in France During the Main German Offensive, 1918*, Angus & Robertson, Sydney, 1937, v. V, p. 580.
34. *Ibid.*, p. 591.
35. Pte J. Ormester, statement, 21 January 1919, AWM 30, B. 6.17 (1)
36. Bean, v. V, p. 592.
37. *Ibid.*, p. 593.
38. *Ibid.*, p. 611.
39. Pte L.F. Hann, statement, 4 September 1918, AWM 30, B 7.2.

Four

1. Lt-Col. H. Sloan, *The Purple and Gold: A History of the 30th Battalion*, Sydney, 1938, p. 182.
2. Lt-Col. K. W. MacKenzie, *The Story of the Seventeenth Battalion AIF in the Great War 1914–1918*, Sydney, 1946, p. 103.
3. *Ibid.*, p. 239.
4. Lt-Col. W. Dollman and Sgt M.M. Skinner, *The Blue and Brown Diamond: A History of the 27th Battalion Australian Imperial force 1915–1919*, Lonnen & Cope, Adelaide, 1921, p. 135.
5. *Ibid.*
6. Pte T.J. Cleary, diary, 24/1/18 cited in Bill Gammage, *The Broken Years: Australian Soldiers in the Great War*, Penguin, Melbourne, 1975, p. 258–9.
7. Eric Fairey, *The 38th Battalion AIF*, Bendigo Advertiser Pty Ltd. and the Cambridge Press, Bendigo, 1920, p. 17, 33.

8. *Ibid.*, p. 45.
9. *The Forty-First: Being a record of the 41st Battalion AIF during the Great War, 1914–18*, p. 92.
10. Newton Wanliss, *The History of the Fourteenth Battalion AIF,* The Arrow Printery, Melbourne, 1929, p. 121.
11. Report to Headquarters 1st Australian Division from 2nd Brigade Headquarters, 1 October 1916, Appendix No. 15.
12. *Ibid.*
13. B. V. Stacy, F.J. Kindon and H.V. Chedgey, *The History of the First Battalion, AIF, 1914–1919*, Sydney, 1931, p. 111.
14. McNicol, p. 238.
15. Captain Walter C. Belford, *Legs–Eleven: Being the story of the 11th Battalion (AIF) in the Great War of 1914–1918,* Imperial Printing Company Ltd., Perth, 1940, p. 280.
16. Wanliss, p. 323–4.
17. Eric Wren, *Randwick to Hargicourt: History of the 3rd Battalion,* Ronald G. McDonald, Sydney, 1935, pp. 196–7.
18. *Ibid.*, p. 196.
19. *Ibid.*, p. 199.
20. Papers of Sgt A.E. Matthews, 3rd Battalion. Copy of diary, p. 7, AWM 2DRL 219.
21. Wren, p. 200.
22. *Ibid.*, p. 261.
23. N.G. McNicol, *The Thirty–Seventh: History of the Thirty-Seventh Battalion AIF,* Modern Printing Co. Pty Ltd, Melbourne, 1936, p. 69. For an account of the shifting emphasis of British training manuals in the evolvement of Australian tactics see, G. E. Mansfield, 'The Importance of Training Manuals in the Improved Combat Performance of the Australian Imperial Force, 1916–1918', Honours thesis, UNE, 2001, *passim*.
24. F.W. Taylor and T.A. Cusack, *Nulli Secundus: A History of the Second Battalion AIF 1914–1919,* Sydney, 1942, p. 283.
25. Keown, p. 272–3.
26. *Ibid.*, p. 280.
27. Major J.E. Lee, *The Chronicle of the 45th Battalion, AIF,* Sydney, 1927, p. 39.
28. A.W. Keown, *Forward with the Fifth,* The Specialty Press, Melbourne, 1921, p. 232.
29. Wanliss, p. 294.
30. *The Forty-First: Being a record of the 41st Battalion AIF during the Great War, 1914–18*, p. 46.

Five

1. Sgt J.M.F. Ryan, statement, 16 December 1918, B10.5, AWM 30.
2. Bean, *Official History of Australia in the War of 1914–18: The AIF in France, During the Main German Offensive, 1918,* v. V, Angus & Robertson, Sydney, 1937, pp. 381, 383.
3. Pte W.P. Seward, statement, 6 December 1918, AWM 30, B. 10. 7
4. Pte L.J. Farrington, statement, 2 March 1918, AWM 30, B. 16.5
5. Sgt C.D. Burton, statement, 11 March 1918, AWM 30, B. 10. 4.
6. CQSM A.L. Guppy, typed extracts from diary, 11 April 1917, AWM 2DRL 447.
7. For a discussion of these points see, Roger Noble, 'Raising the White Flag: The Surrender of Australian Soldiers on the Western Front', *Revue Internationale d'Histoire Militaire*, n. 72, 1990.

8. Private L.C. Gillan, statement, 3 December 1918, AWM 30, B 6.16 (1).
9. L/Sgt. A L. Harrison, statement, 23 April, 1919, AWM 30, B. 14.1.
10. Pte P.J. Gill, statement, 6 December 1918, AWM 30, B. 14.1.
11. Cpl. J.E. Morris, statement, AWM 30, B. 14.1.
12. Sgt W. Chappell, statement, 31 December 1918, AWM 30, B 6.11 (1) and (2).
13. Pte R.F. Starr, Pte J.C. Anderson, Pte Walter Green, statement, 12 December 1918, AWM 30, B. 11.1
14. Sapper E.J. Long, Sapper C. W. Morris, statements, 13 December 1918, AWM 30, B. 5.54
15. Capt. D.P. Wells, statement, 30 December 1918, AWM 30, B. 13.5
16. Pte W.J. Baldock, statement, 21 December 1918, AWM 30, B6.16 (1).
17. Pte R. E. Membrey, statement 29 January 1918, AWM 30, B6.16 (1).
18. Capt. J. H. Honeysett, narrative, AWM 3DRL 4043, 1 of 3, pp. 15–6.
19. Papers of Lt V. Garnet Veness, diary, 11 April 1917, AWM PR 01059 1 of 2.
20. Cpl L.R. Dawes, typed narrative, AWM, PRO 000140, pp. 2–3.
21. Lt N.D.L. Cumming, statement, 12 July 1918, AWM 30, B. 17.5
22. Cpl H. Ford letter to Sgt. W. C. Groves, 17 September 1930 in Sgt W C. Groves, AWM 2DRL 268.
23. Pte K.S. Ross, statement, 28 February 1919, AWM 30, B. 5.44.
24. Pte A.D. Stone, statement, 23 January 1919, AWM 30, B. 16.11
25. Cpl A. McKee, statement, 17 December 1918, AWM 30, B 14.5.
26. Statement of Ptes Gigg, Carter, Fairwether, Brown, AWM 30, B 14.5.
27. Pte H.R. Putt, statement, 23 December 1918, AWM 30, B. 11.3.
28. Pte S.F. Cubis, statement, 4 July 1918, AWM 30, B. 6.5 (1). Underline in the original.
29. Pte P.J. Liddy, statement, 17 December 1918, AWM 30, B. 10.13
30. Pte H. West, undated statement, AWM 30, B. 11.3
31. Papers of F. Klingner, diary, AWM PR 91/099.
32. Sgt L. Ramshaw, statement, 12 February 1918, AWM 30, B. 11.3
33. Pte J.A. O'Rourke, statement, 24 October 1918, B10. 5, AWM 30.
34. Pte Victor Savage, statement, 19 November 1918, B.10. 5, AWM 30.
35. Sgt J.S. Tomlinson, statement, 23 January 1918, AWM 30, B. 13. 18
36. Pte A.T. Nelligan, statement, 6 March 1918, AWM 30, B. 16.11
37. Pte A.E. Park, statement, 16 December 1918, AWM 30, B. 11.3
38. Bean, v. V, p. 396–7 n. 67.
39. Pte L.J. Briand, statement, 13 February 1918, AWM 30, B. 13. 22
40. Lt O. Flight, statement, 27 December 1918, AWM 30, B. 3.6. Destruction of one's machine was standard practice it would seem. See statement by Lt F.B. Willmott, 18 December 1918, B. 3.17.
41. Pte James Egan, statement, 11 December 1918, AWM 30, B. 17.3
42. Pte Thomas Bolton, statement, AWM 30, B. 16.1
43. Gretchen Kewley, *Humanitarian Law in Armed Conflicts*, VCTA Publishing, Collingwood, 1984, p. 7.

44. Honeysett, narrative, p. 17.
45. Capt. D.P. Wells, statement, 30 December 1918, AWM 30, B. 13.5
46. Cpl L.D. Brooks, statement, 21 January 1919, AWM 30, B. 6.18.
47. Neil Pilford, "Controversy over the use of dum dum bullets in the First World War, in *Imperial War Museum Review, No 5*, pp. 101–2.
48. Pte G. Abbott, statement, 24 December 1918, AWM 30, B. 6.7 (1).
49. Pte C.H.E. Duncan, statement, 21 December 1918, AWM 30, B. 6.16 (1).
50. Pte William Quinn, statement, 12 November 1918, AWM 30, B 14.1.
51. See for example statements by Pte A.B. Rankine, 30 November 1918 and Pte H. Crossley, 20 January 1918 in AWM 30, B 14.1.
52. Pte B.J. Healy, statement, 28 August 1918, AWM 30, B. 11.3
53. Pte L. Gosewinckel, statement, 5 February 1918, AWM 30, B. 5.14
54. Pte W. Birch, statement, 2 December 1918, AWM 30, B. 17.12
55. Pte W.R. Hobson, undated statement, AWM 30, B. 8.4
56. Cpl W. Stuart, statement, 3 December 1918, AWM 30, B. 6.1 (1)
57. Pte C.H. Kennedy, statement, 2 December 1918, AWM 30, B5.15B
58. L/Cpl F. Peachy, undated statement, AWM 30, B. 13. 18
59. Pte A.T. Nelligan, statement, 6 March 1918, AWM 30, B. 16.11
60. Archie Barwick, Diary No. 4, cited in Bill Gammage, *The Broken Years: Australian Soldiers in the Great War*, Penguin, Melbourne, 1975, p. 258.
61. Cpl D.W. Austin, statement, 12 November 1918, AWM 30, B. 6.14 (2)
62. Pte C.J. Conley; Pte T. Hodgson, statement, 22 January 1919, AWM 30, B. 10. 13
63. Pte George Hilton, statement, 11 February 1918, AWM 30, B. 6.16 (1).
64. Pte A.E. Hatchard, statement, 5 February 1918, AWM 30, B. 6.16 (1).
65. Pte L.J. Kinna, statement, 20 December 1918, AWM 30, B. 10.7. The buried man was Pte E. Westergard, 48th Bn.
66. Capt. D.P. Wells, statement, 30 December 1918, AWM 30, B. 13.5
67. Lt William Stones, statement, 11 April 1919, AWM 30, B. 13.5
68. AWM 27, 424/13.
69. Sgt J.C. Whitbread, statement, 13 December 1918; Pte. W. J. Jones, statement, 6 December 1918, AWM 30, B. 13.5
70. Pte John Bolton, statement, 4 July 1918, AWM 30, B. 16.7
71. Pte A.A. Stephens, statement, 27 September 1917, AWM, B. 13.9
72. Cpl L.R. Dawes, narrative, AWM, PRO 000814, p. 39.
73. Papers of Cpl Harry Andrew Still, AWM, PR00753, [1 of 3].

Six

1. Rosalind Crone, 'In the Hands of the Hun: Australian Prisoners of the Germans in the Great War', unpublished paper, Australian War Memorial, 2002, p. 1.
2. See account of Pte. Raymond Thomas Ayres, PR 89/136, 89/14/15.
3. Crone, *op. cit.*, p. 10.
4. Statement, Pte L.W. Keirnan, 54 Bn, AWM 30, B 14.5.

5. Papers of Cpl Harry Andrew Still, AWM, PR00753, [1 of 3].
6. *Ibid., passim.*
7. David Chalk, 'Talks with old "Gerfangers"', *Journal of the Australian War Memorial*, n. 14, April 1989, p. 19.
8. Statement, Pte Frank Comery, 16 Bn, AWM 30, B. 13.22

Conclusion

1. David Grossman, *On Killing: The Psychological Cost of Learning to Kill in War and Society*, Little Brown and Company, New York, 1995, pp. 180–1.
2. *Ibid.*, p. 181.
3. Bean, v. I, pp. 606–7.
4. Grossman, p. 124.
5. Bill Gammage, *The Broken Years: Australian Soldiers in the Great War*, Penguin, Melbourne, 1975, p. 259.
6. Grossman., pp. xi–xxxiv, 249–332.
7. Cpl W.D. Gallwey, letter, 2/8/17 cited in Gammage, p. 259.
8. Dale Blair, *Dinkum Diggers: An Australian Battalion at War*, Melbourne University Press, 2001, p. 144.
9. For Grossman's discussion of this experiment see pp. 141–5, 187–8.
10. Niall Ferguson, *The Pity of War*, Penguin Books, London, 1998, pp. 368–71, 388.

Bibliography

Official Histories

C.E.W. Bean, *Official History of Australia in the War of 1914–18: The Story of Anzac: The First Phase*, v. I, Angus & Robertson, Sydney, 1941, 12th edition [1921].

—, *Official History of Australia in the War of 1914–18: The Story of Anzac: From 4 May 1915 to the Evacuation*, v. II, Angus & Robertson, Sydney, 1936 fourth edition [1924].

—, *Official History of Australia in the War of 1914–18: The AIF in France 1916*, v. III, Angus & Robertson, Sydney, 1936 [1929].

—, *Official History of Australia in the War of 1914–18: The AIF in France 1917*, v. IV, Angus & Robertson, Sydney, 1933.

—, *Official History of Australia in the War of 1914–18: The AIF in France, During the Main German Offensive, 1918*, v. V, Angus & Robertson, Sydney, 1937.

Unit histories

Dollman, Lt-Col. W. and Skinner, Sgt M.M., *The Blue and Brown Diamond: A History of the 27th Battalion Australian Imperial force 1915–1919*, Lonnen & Cope, Adelaide, 1921.

Fairey, Eric, *The 38th Battalion AIF*, Bendigo Advertiser Pty Ltd and the Cambridge Press, Bendigo, 1920.

Gorman, Captain E., *With the Twenty-Second: A History of the 22nd Battalion, AIF*, H.H. Champion, Australasian Authors' Agency, Melbourne, 1919.

Keown, W., *Forward with the Fifth*, The Specialty Press, Melbourne, 1921.

Lee, Major J.E., *The Chronicle of the 45th Battalion, AIF*, Sydney, 1927.

MacKenzie, Lt-Col. K.W., *The Story of the Seventeenth Battalion AIF in the Great War 1914–1918*, Sydney, 1946.

McNicol, N.G., *The Thirty-Seventh: History of the Thirty-Seventh Battalion AIF*, Modern Printing Co. Pty Ltd, Melbourne, 1936.

Sloan, Lt-Col. H., *The Purple and Gold: A History of the 30th Battalion*, Sydney, 1938.

Stacy, B.V. Kindon, F.J. and Chedgey, H.V., *The History of the First Battalion, AIF, 1914–1919*, Sydney, 1931.

Taylor, F. W. and Cusack, T. A., *Nulli Secundus: A History of the Second Battalion AIF 1914–1919*, Sydney, 1942.

Wanliss, Newton, *The History of the Fourteenth Battalion AIF*, The Arrow Printery, Melbourne, 1929.

Belford, Captain Walter C., *Legs-Eleven: Being the Story of the 11th Battalion (AIF) in the Great War of 1914–1918*, Imperial Printing Company Ltd, Perth, 1940.

Wren, Eric, *Randwick to Hargicourt: History of the 3rd Battalion*, Ronald G. McDonald, Sydney, 1935.

The Forty-First: Being a record of the 41st Battalion AIF during the Great War, 1914–18.

Books

Blair, Dale, *Dinkum Diggers: An Australian Battalion at War*, Melbourne University Press, 2001.

Bourke, Joanna, *An Intimate History of Killing: Face-to-face Killing in Twentieth Century Warfare*, Granta Books, London, 1999.

Carthew, Noel, *Voices from the Trenches: Letters to Home*, New Holland Publishers, Sydney, 2002.

Charlton, Peter, *Pozières*.

Clausewitz, Carl von, *On War*, Penguin Classics, 1968 [1832].

Corfield, Robin S, *Don't forget me, cobber: The Battle of Fromelles 19/20 July 1916: An Enquiry*, Corfield and Company, Rosanna, Victoria, 2000.

Dennis, Peter, et al, *The Oxford Companion to Australian Military History*, Oxford University Press, Melbourne, 1995.

Ferguson, Niall, *The Pity of War*, Penguin Books, London, 1998.

Fewster, Kevin, *Gallipoli Correspondent: the frontline diary of C.E.W. Bean*, Allen & Unwin, Sydney, 1983.

Grossman, David, *On Killing: The Psychological Cost of learning to Kill in War and Society*, Little Brown Books, New York, 1996.

Joynt, W.D., *Breaking the Road for the Rest*, Hyland House, Melbourne, 1979.

Keegan, John, *The Face of Battle*, Jonathan Cape, London, 1976.

Kerr, Greg, *Lost Anzacs: The Story of Two Brothers*, Oxford University Press, Melbourne, 1997.

Kewley, Gretchen, *Humanitarian Law in Armed Conflicts*, VCTA Publishing, Melbourne, 1984.

International Law Concerning the Conduct of Hostilities: Collection of Hague Conventions and Some Other Treaties, International Committee of the Red Cross, Geneva, 1989.

Gammage, Bill, *The Broken Years: Australian Soldiers in the Great War*, Penguin, Melbourne, 1975.

McMullin, Ross, *Pompey Elliott*, Scribe Publications, Melbourne, 2002.

Monash, John, *The Australian Victories in France in 1918*, The Lothian Book Publishing Company, Melbourne, 1923 [1920].

Schuler, Phillip, *Australia in Arms: A Narrative of the Australasian Imperial Force and their achievement at Anzac*, London, T. Fisher Unwin, 1916.

Wells, Donald A., *The Laws of Land Warfare: A Guide to U.S. Army Manuals*, Greenwood Press, Westport, Connecticut, 1992.

Articles

Chalk, David, 'Talks with old "Gerfangeners"', *Journal of the Australian War Memorial*, no. 14, April 1989.

Pilford, Neil, 'Controversy over the use of dum dum bullets in the First World War', *Imperial War Museum Review*, no. 5.

Crone, Rosalind, 'In the Hands of the Hun: Australian Prisoners of the Germans in the Great War', unpublished paper, Australian War Memorial, 2002.

Roger Noble, 'Raising the White Flag: The Surrender of Australian Soldiers on the Western Front', *Revue Internationale d'Histoire Militaire*, no. 72, 1990.

Theses

G.E. Mansfield, 'The Importance of Training Manuals in the Improved Combat Performance of the Australian Imperial Force, 1916–1918', Honours thesis, UNE, 2001.

Primary Sources

AWM Record Groups

AWM 27 – Subject classified files.
AWM 30 – Repatriated Prisoner of War statements.

AWM Personal Records

Ayres, Pte R.T., AWM PR 89/136.
Creedon, Pte D.B., AWM 1DRL 223.
Dawes, Cpl L.R., AWM, PRO 000140.
Groves, Sgt W.C., AWM 2DRL 268.
Guppy, CQSM A.L., AWM 2DRL 447.
Honeysett, Capt J.H., AWM 3DRL 4043.
Klingner, F., AWM PR 91/099.
Still, Cpl H.A., AWM, PR00753.
Veness, Lt V. Garnet, AWM PR 01059.

Newspapers/magazines

Bulletin.

Index

Names

Abbot, Pte G. 65
Alexander II, Czar 19
Augustine, St 16
Austin, Cpl D.W. 67
Baldock, Pte W.J. 58
Barwick, Archie 66
Bean, C.E.W. 7, 8, 9, 12, 13, 23, 24, 25, 77, 78, 83, 84
Blacket, Lt 'Joe' 45
Bolton, Pte John 69
Bolton, Pte Thomas 64
Bourke, Joanna 21, 32, 84
Briand, Pte L.J. 63
Brooks, Cpl L.D. 64
Brown, L/Cpl 60
Burton, Sgt C.D. 55
Chappell, Sgt W. 57
Charlton, Peter 9
Clausewitz, Carl von 17
Comery, Pte Frank 75
Creedon, Pte D.B. 27
Crone, Rosalind 71, 72, 74
Crooks, CSM 51
Cubis, Pte S.F. 60
Cumming, Lt N.D.L. 59
Curtis, Pte F. 62
Dawes, Cpl L.R. 59, 69
Dunant, Henri 18, 36, 68
Duncan, Pte C.H.E. 65
Egan, Pte James 63
Elliot, Brig. Gen. 'Pompey' 12
Farrington, Pte L.J. 54
Ferguson, Niall 82

Flight, Lt O. 63
Ford, Cpl H. 59
Foss, Capt. Maitland 33
Garnet Veness, Lt V. 59
Gellibrand, Brig. Gen. John 12, 13
Gill, Pte P.J. 57
Gosewinckel, Pte L. 65
Graves, Robert 12
Grossman, David 32, 77, 78, 79, 84
Guppy, CQMS A.L. 55
Haig, General Sir Douglas 30
Handcock, Lt Peter 13
Hann, Pte L.F. 42
Harburn, Capt. 'Billy' 41
Harrison, L/Sgt A.L. 56
Healy, Pte B.J. 65
Heane, Brig. Gen. 50
Hilton, Pte George 67
Hird, Capt. 54
Holmes, Richard 79, 84
Honeysett, Capt. J.H. 21, 58, 64
Howell-Price, Lt-Col. 49
Jackson, Maj. I. 25
Jobson, Brig. Gen. Alexander 12
Joynt, Capt. W.D. 8
Keegan, John 8, 9, 77, 79, 84
Keirnan, Pte L.W. 72
Kennedy, Pte C.H. 41, 66
Kerr, Cpl George 25
Kinna, Pte L.J. 68
Klingner, Pte F. 61
Laing, Lt 37
Larkin, Sgt E.R. 24
Lieber, Prof. Francis 18

Loveday, Lt 49
Love, Pte 54
Mackay, Iven 9
Marshall, S.L.A. 79
Matthews, Sgt A.E. 49
McCay, Maj. Gen. J.W. 36, 37
McGrath, Cpl 54
McKee, Cpl 60
Meaker, Pte 49
Membrey, Pte R.E. 58
Milgram, Stanley 80
Mills, Capt. C. 35
Monash, Gen. Sir John 12, 23
Moore, Capt. F.L. 8, 12
Morant, Lt Harry 'Breaker' 13
Morris, Cpl J.E. 57
Morrison, Sgt 51
Mortimer, Capt. 36
Mueller, Uber Lt 74
Murdoch, Maj. A.W. 36
Nelligan, Pte A.T. 62, 66
O'Rourke, Pte J.A. 62
Park, Pte A.E. 63
Putt, Pte H.R. 60
Quinn, Pte William 65
Ralphs, Pte E.C. 45, 56
Ramshaw, Sgt L. 61
Ransom, Capt. 57
Rolls, Lt 54
Ross, Pte K.S. 60
Ryan, Sgt J.F. 54
Sanders, Reg 75
Saundercock, Pte A.R. 45
Savage, Pte Victor 62
Seward, Pte W.P. 54, 68
Simpson, Lt 42, 67
Stephens, Pte A.A. 69
Still, Cpl Harry Andrew 70, 73, 74
Stone, Pte A.D. 60
Stones, Lt W. 68
Stuart, Cpl 66
Swank and Marchand 77, 79

Textor, Johan 16
Thompson, Lt Harold 48
Tomlinson, Sgt T.S. 62
Vattel, Emmerich 17
Wanliss, Newton 46
Weger, Pte 48, 49
Wells, Capt. D.P. 64, 68
Wells, Donald 16
West, Pte 54
West, Pte H. 61
Wheeler, Jim 75
Whitelaw, Lt 39
Wolff, Christian 16
Yorke, Sgt 49

Places
Gallipoli
400 Plateau 24
Ari Burnu 24
Hell's Spit 25
Hill 971 25
Little Ari Burnu 25
McCay's Hill 26
North Beach 24
Pine Ridge 25, 26, 38
Quinn's Post 27
Razorback, the 26

Western Front
Armentières 30, 66
Bapaume 65
Bayonet Trench 48
Bois Grenier 67, 69
Bullecourt 21, 39, 55, 59, 61, 62, 63, 67, 68, 72, 75
Cambrai 66
Dernancourt 54, 61
Dulmen 73
Flers 80
Fort MacDonald 72
Fromelles (Fleurbaix) 34, 35, 36, 56, 60, 61, 63, 65, 66, 70, 72, 73

Glencorse Wood 51
Hangard Wood 65
Hollebeke 54
Houplines 66
Lagnicourt 60
Laventie 57
Lille 65, 72
Menin Road 40
Messines 52
Minden 74
Mouquet Farm 41, 58, 63, 67
Mourlancourt 12
Noreuil 39, 57, 59
Passchendaele 8, 12
Pozières 7, 8, 9, 12, 37, 48
Soltan 74
Sunray Trench 39
Verdun 30
Villers-Bretonneux 41, 42
Vitoria 16
Warlancourt 57
Warneton 46
Ypres 50, 64

Units

Divisions
4th Division 46
5th Australian Division 34
5th Division 36

Brigades
2nd Australian Infantry Brigade 46
3rd Australian Infantry Brigade 26
3rd NZ Infantry Brigade 34
9th Australian Infantry Brigade 12

Battalions
1st Battalion 24, 47, 66, 80
2nd Battalion 30, 50
3rd Battalion 30, 48, 49, 50, 52, 80
4th Battalion 9
5th Battalion 8, 51
7th Battalion 47
8th Battalion 8, 47
8th Machine-gun Battalion 36
9th Battalion 25
10th Battalion 24
11th Battalion 48, 60
12th Battalion 37
13th Battalion 68
14th Battalion 25, 48, 51
15th Battalion 66
16th Battalion 75
17th Battalion 44, 61
20th Battalion 67
21st Battalion 41, 58
22nd Battalion 22, 59
23rd Battalion 65
25th Battalion 66
26th Battalion 33, 60
27th Battalion 45
28th Battalion 57
29th Battalion 36, 39
30th Battalion 44
32nd Battalion 62
33rd Battalion 42
37th Battalion 46, 48, 50
38th Battalion 46, 66
41st Battalion 46
45th Battalion 51
46th Battalion 39, 55
48th Battalion 38, 39, 61, 67, 68, 75
50th Battalion 57
51st Battalion 41, 60, 61, 65
53rd Battalion 35, 56, 57, 65
54th Battalion 54, 60, 72
60th Battalion 42

Others
1st Field Ambulance 69
4th Australian Divisional School 21
4th Light Trench Mortar Battery 4
Bush Veldt Carbineers 14
No. 2 Squadron, AFC 63

www.ingramcontent.com/pod-product-compliance
Lightning Source LLC
Chambersburg PA
CBHW030913080526
44589CB00010B/283